# The Farmer
# and the Goose with the
# Golden Eyes

*The farmhouse at Little Stoke, with Edward and Margaret
Davis and their five children,
photographed in 1907*

From Little Stoke Farm to Slimbridge

# The Farmer
## and the
# Goose
## with the
# Golden Eyes

## Martin Davis

A celebration in words and pictures of a vanished part of
south Gloucestershire, and the founding of the
Wildfowl and Wetland Trust

 redcliffe

First published in 2009

ISBN  978-1-906593-37-7

Published by Redcliffe Press, www.redcliffepress.co.uk
Design and layout by Martin Davis
Printed and bound by  HSW Print, Tonypandy, Rhondda


Publication of this book has been made possible with grants from:

Dedicated to the memory of my father

# HOWARD HENRY DAVIS

Farmer, Ornithologist

and Conservationist

# Farms around Stoke Gifford, Gloucestershire in the 1830s

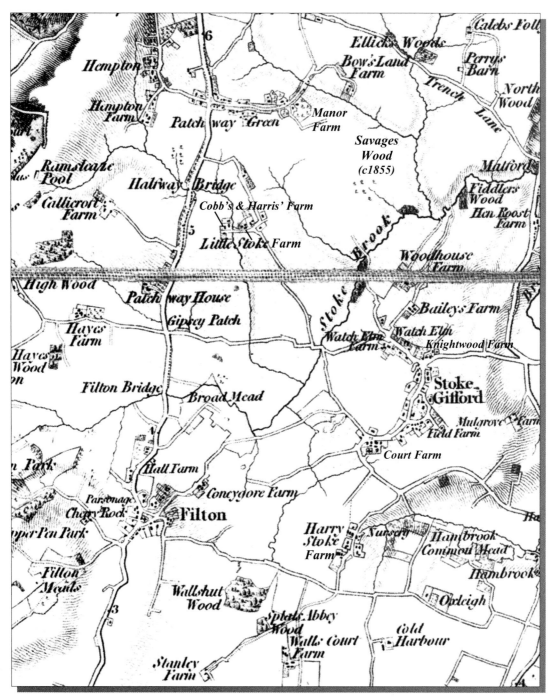

*Map showing the farms in the Stoke Gifford area, with additional farms mentioned in this book.*
*Reproduced from the 1830 Ordnance Survey map.*

# Contents

# Acknowledgements

I am very grateful to Lady Philippa Scott for her interest in this book, for writing a foreward, for granting me permission to reproduce some original sketches by Sir Peter Scott, and allowing me to include a quotation from his autobiography, *The Eye of the Wind*. I also extend my thanks to Joe Blossom, who has a long association with the Wildlife and Wetlands Trust, for providing a recent photograph that he took of a Lesser Whitefront goose at Slimbridge. I also acknowledge the help given by John Creedon of the Trust.

I would like to thank the Duke of Beaufort and his Estate staff for their assistance in the production of this book.

Roger James, Community Relations Manager at Rolls-Royce plc, in Patchway, deserves particular thanks for his enthusiastic interest. Roger introduced me to members of the Rolls-Royce Heritage Trust, who were most helpful, searching through its extensive archives for photographs of the aero-engine developments on former Little Stoke farmland. Through this Trust I also met local historian, Jackie Sims, who made some invaluable suggestions to improve the book's content.

Members of the Town Councils of Bradley Stoke and Patchway, together with Stoke Gifford Parish Council have all shown interest in the book, and I thank them for their encouragement. All three Councils and Rolls-Royce plc have provided welcome financial support, without which this book could not have been published. Because of this, profits from the sales of the book will be shared between the Wildfowl and Wetlands Trust, Three Brooks Conservation Group, Patchway Conservation Group and Southern Brooks Community Partnership. My thanks, too, to John Morris, of Wild Spaces, for his interest in the conservation aspects.

Mike Stanbrook, who has extensively researched the history of Stoke Gifford, has made available photographs and documents, for which I am grateful. Madeleine Gill and Andrew Newton are also thanked for providing many details of the three generations of the Player family of Stoke Gifford. Further thanks to Adrian Kerton who has an extensive website devoted to the long history of Stoke Gifford.

My thanks, too, to an old school friend, Alan Holzer, who has written about his recollection of eight weeks he spent at Little Stoke Farm in 1944. I also extend my thanks to John Penny, author of *Bristol at War*, who provided detailed information about the air raids in the early 1940s.

I am thankful, too, for the professional guidance received from Barbara Cooper in London, Paul Harding in Kent and, during the final stages of the book's evolution, from Clara and John Sansom of Redcliffe Press, based in Bristol. My thanks, as well, to Pat and Gerry Arnold for their considerable interest and help.

Peter Towey provided most welcome and much needed corrections to my attempts to transcribe the 15th century petition reproduced on pages 8 and 9.

I have endeavoured to obtain permission to reproduce any material that might be protected by copyright law. If something has slipped through, I apologise. Should the book run to a second edition, the matter will be corrected.

Janet Thawley and Dorothy Burden, grand-daughters of Harry Ponting, who worked on the farm for many years, have kindly let me include some of their photographs and an extract from the shepherd's logbook belonging to their grandfather; for which I am very grateful.

My thanks to Jim and Betty Wyatt, who worked at the farm from 1947, and to Phyllis Knapp, who remembers life on the farm well before the Second World War, with admirable clarity. I extend my thanks, too, to all the descendants of the Cutler, Williams, Weaver and Knapp families. Without the interest and enthusiasm they have shown, this book may not have been completed. I also offer my thanks to Alf Hargreave, who remembers the former Little Stoke well, for his help contacting many of the above family members.

And lastly I am particularly grateful for the encouragement and help I received in this venture from my wife, Elizabeth.

Martin Davis

*Sketch of a Pink Headed Duck by Peter Scott, 1947.*

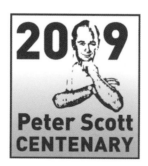

# Foreword

It was an excellent idea of Martin's to write a book about his father, Howard Davis. It is particularly apposite that it should come out in Peter Scott's centenary year. For it was Howard who was largely responsible for the creation of what was ultimately to become the Wildfowl & Wetlands Trust at Slimbridge.

In 1945 Howard invited Peter to come and look at the large flock of European White-fronted geese on the salt marsh at Slimbridge. Among those 2000 White-fronts Peter found a bird which he had hoped might be there — a Lesser White-fronted goose — and it was only the second on record for Britain. Not only was there one but two.

Peter wrote in his book *Observations of Wildlife*:

'As well as the Lesser White-fronts, we saw six other species on that day and as we returned up the muddy lane from the salt marsh, I decided that here was the place in which to establish the new research station which I had been planning for so long'.

Philippa Scott
Honorary Director, WWT

# Prologue

This is the story of a farm that vanished to make way for modern housing. It is the story of both one particular farm and of every farm that has similarly vanished — thousands of them across the country. Words and pictures, plus a little history about a particular Gloucestershire farm, are used to celebrate the loss of a way of life and the lost heritage that stretches back over many centuries.

The impetus for this book initially came from two sources. The first was a recently discovered old Ovaltine tin, full of negatives of scenes around Little Stoke before the Second World War. Most were taken with a Kodak bellows camera. Handled well, it produced good photographs that were sharp to the edges. Some others, less sharp, were most probably taken using an old box camera, with a fixed focus lens. Some negatives were in pristine condition and others scratched, stretching back to before 1920. I already had well over 100 photographs taken on Little Stoke Farm in the 1950s; some I took, with a newly acquired 35mm camera; but the majority were taken by my mother with a second hand Leica. I also had many photographs that were taken in the 1940s, again by my mother, using a Rolleiflex camera.

The second impetus came from the interest shown, by a packed audience at the library in Patchway, just north of Bristol, when I was invited to talk about Little Stoke Farm. It was particularly rewarding to find descendants of some of the families that once lived and worked on the farm in the audience.

The farm has, of course, disappeared under the houses of the modern Little Stoke, the growing town of Bradley Stoke as well as Rolls-Royce plc. Hardly anything of the farm remains, and its history and way of life will, all too easily, be forgotten. This book is intended to redress the balance.

I have not attempted to write a formal history of Little Stoke. Instead I have brought together a mixture of memories and impressions, illustrated with more than 150 photographs, maps and a few paintings. Some historical details are included to help to set the Little Stoke of the early-20th century into context: to show how farming life there evolved. My primary purpose is to give the reader some insight into what it was like to live, and in my case, to grow up, on a typical farm in the Gloucestershire Severn Vale.

At a deeper level this book is about two matters that I believe to be important, ones that are not confined to just a few hundred acres of what was once south Gloucestershire countryside. Both these matters are, in a sense, universal. They challenge the way we think about our environments.

The first is about the loss of our heritage and history as cities expand. This can result in the complete obliteration of a way of life that has evolved over 1,000 or more years. The destruction, for that is what it was, of Little Stoke Farm, is but one example of so-called progress that will have been replicated around just about every city in the land. Handled well with a full knowledge of local history, the urbanisation of the landscape could and should be achieved with far greater sensitivity: a true integration of the new with the old. At no time in our history is this more urgent than now. As an island we are over-populated, and we have insufficient housing for the ever-growing number of people. Despite the onset of the economic downturn that became increasingly apparent in 2008, the need for housing will remain. How this is fulfilled needs much more careful forethought and planning than has often been applied. My story, therefore, is not only about the fate of a particular farm, but also about every farm in lowland England that has to make way for housing and industry.

The second is about human endeavour: a lifelong commitment by an individual, in this case to nature conservation, can set in motion a chain of events of national and international importance. As is revealed later in this book, my father, Howard Davis, who lived at Little Stoke and farmed there, held such a passion — for the preservation of the natural world. This led to his pivotal part in the creation of the (then) Severn Wildfowl Trust at Slimbridge. Were he alive today he would have given his full support to the groups — Three Brooks Nature Conservation Group, The Green Gym and Wild Spaces — that strive to conserve and enhance the remaining wildlife spaces in and around Little Stoke and Bradley Stoke.

Returning, then, to both Little Stoke and Bradley Stoke; those living in the houses built during the past 20 or 30 years on the farmland and who have stayed, will be putting down their own roots, just as I did some seventy years ago. In time these new roots will join those of the past generations that lived in the small, once rural hamlet of Little Stoke which, surprisingly, supported as many as five farms around 250 and more years ago.

Some, who lived and grew up in the old Little Stoke, have described it to me as a special place, as they recall walks across the fields, and the community of families in the cluster of houses that stood around the farm.

In writing this book I have had the pleasure of long, rose tinted conversations, after far too many years, with some of those who once lived on the farm and with their descendants; hours of wonderful recollections. I am particularly grateful to them for their time and interest.

Martin Davis, July 2009

# From the Domesday Book, 1086

*The Land of Osbern Giffard in Gloucestershire as recorded in the Domesday Book. (Lines 6-8 relate to Stoke Gifford - Stoche, as it then was).*

**In "LETBERG" Hundred:**

**The same Osbern holds STOKE GIFFORD. There are 5 hides paying geld. Dunn held it. In demesne are 4 ploughs; and 8 villans and 3 bordars and a priest with 8 ploughs. There are 4 slaves. It was worth 6l; now 8l.**

*[Reproduced with permission of the National Archives].*

**Hide**: *area of land between 60 and 120 acres;* **Geld**: *tax paid to the crown;* **Demesne**: *land owned by the landlord;* **Plough**: *the area that a plough pulled by eight oxen could cover in a day;* **Villans**: *peasants;* **Bordars**: *peasants of a lower rank;* **6l**: *£6.*

# Chapter 1

# Little Stoke

Little Stoke, with the larger Great Stoke, which was occupied in Roman times, and the hamlet of Harry Stoke, together formed the once rural village of Stoke Gifford. The name Great Stoke has fallen out of use, while that of Stoke Gifford is usually applied to the area formerly covered by Great Stoke. The original village of Great Stoke, then called Stoche, is mentioned in the Domesday Book. Perhaps a dozen people lived there in 1086. The five hides and 12 ploughs of land around the village equate to about 2000 acres in modern terms.

The Church will have played its role: the Domesday Book records that there was a priest in Saxon Stoche before the Norman Conquest. It is still possible to follow an old Saxon pathway that ran from Stoke Gifford towards Patchway Common, cutting its way across land that later became the future Little Stoke Farm.

After the Conquest the Manor was granted, by William the Conquerer, to Osbern Giffard, whose ancestors were the Lords of Longueville-la-Giffard, in Normandy. The Giffards held Stoche until early 1322, when Baron John Giffard, who had rebelled against Edward II, was hanged in Gloucester. This part of South Gloucestershire will have had a rich human history, extending back over 1000 years. Much of this would have involved the land and its uses.

Harry Stoke, called Estoch in the Domesday Book, was then part of lands owned by the Bishop of Coutances, in Normandy. Locally it was held by Theobald on the bishop's behalf. There were two hides and two ploughs of land (about 500 acres), one hide paid tax, the other did not. The landlord held one plough of land, a smallholder another plough. There were two other villagers and six slaves and a five acre (hay) meadow. As Harry Stoke is only a short walk, south, from Great Stoke, the 2000 acres of Stoche land must have extended more to the north of the village, land that was later to form Watch Elm and Woodhouse Farms, as well as Bailey's Court and Little Stoke Farm.

*Stoke Park House, home of the local Berkeley family. Engraving by J. Walker, 1798.*

In 1086 Stoche lay in the administrative area known as Letberg HD (Ledbury Hundred), a small narrow area extending from the village towards, but not quite reaching Redeuuiche (Redwick) on the banks of the Severn. Estoch (Harry Stoke) was then in the neighbouring Hundred of Sineshovedes (Swinehead). Early nineteenth century maps show that the Letberg countryside was still open farmland, with scattered farmsteads, and few villages and hamlets: Great Stoke, Little Stoke and Over. The Domesday Book has only two entries for the Ledbury Hundred: Stoche and the smaller Lee, which was centred on the hamlet of Over and its manor. In 1086 Lee, like Harry Stoke, belonged to the Bishop of Coutances, and was held on his behalf by Robert of Doynton: before 1066 it had been held by a Saxon, called Algar. It comprised just one hide, which paid tax, and one plough of land. There were three smallholders and two slaves. Little Stoke is not mentioned, farmsteads there then would have been part of Osbern Giffard's Manor at Stoche.

The parish land of Stoke Gifford came under the ownership of Maurice de Berkeley in 1337. In the 1550s, descendants of Maurice, built and lived in the Elizabethan Stoke Park House that stood to the south of Stoke Gifford on a bluff overlooking the city of Bristol. The present house was rebuilt in the mid 1700s.

Some of the Stoke Gifford Berkeleys served their country with distinction; none more so than Sir Richard Berkeley, knighted by Elizabeth I, who held various important posts, including Lieutenant of the Tower of London. His son, Maurice, was also knighted. In 1740, Maurice's direct descendant, Elizabeth Symes, married Charles Noel, Duke of Beaufort. From then until 1915, the parish belonged to the Beaufort family at Badminton, in Gloucestershire. Before 1915, when the Beaufort Estate sold its holdings in and around Stoke Gifford, generations of local farmers had, since 1740, paid their dues and fulfilled their contractual obligations, to a succession of Lords of the Manor at Badminton House.

W.G. Hoskins, in his book *The Making of the English Landscape*, writes that almost all the villages that now exist, did so at the time of the Domesday survey. The notable exceptions being those places that grew up as part of the Industrial Revolution in the 18th and 19th centuries, and, of course, new towns such as Bradley Stoke. In 1086 the population of England was around one and a quarter million. The great majority lived in small villages, hamlets and farms, spread across the countryside. Over three quarters of the land that was farmed around 1900 was already being farmed at the time of the Domesday Book. Despite periods of hardship, over time the Saxons became good, well-organised farmers: it was they who felled most of the woodland trees east of the Severn. About one third of all the land they cleared was arable, while a quarter was meadow and pasture. At the time of the Norman invasion, a third more of Gloucestershire farmland was used for growing cereals than in 1950. A summer walk along the Saxon pathway from Stoke Gifford towards Patchway Common may well have been through large fields, perhaps between 80 and 200 acres each, of wheat and other crops, and pastureland with sheep, goats and cattle. A few old hedgerows that now thread their way between rows of houses in Bradley Stoke may, therefore, be 1000 years old, however most were planted later, when the common land was enclosed.

A map (see Appendix 1), researched and drawn by Mike Stanbrook, shows the Stoke Gifford Manors in the mid-1300s. The land, which later became Little Stoke Farm, comprised four large fields. There were four dwellings at Little Stoke, possibly the homes of small-holders, tenant farmers of parts of the large common field system. About half the land of the future Bailey's Court Farm was woodland.

By 1500 the population of England had grown to about 3 million. The landscape changed in the 400 years that followed the Norman Conquest. Norman castles, such as at Berkeley and Bristol, ensured a firm grip on the county. Villages grew in

*1471-1483: A petition by Humphrey and Sybil Forster, of Little Stoke, to the Prince of Wales, Edward Plantagenet, King Edward IV's eldest son. Reproduced courtesy of The National Archives, Kew. [The author's full transcription is in Appendix 2, pages 125/6]*

size and many churches were built. Sheep became the most abundant livestock: around five for each man, woman and child by the end of the 15th century. Wool production and cloth weaving had significantly enhanced the wealth of many people across the county. It is most probable that the small-holders at Little Stoke, throughout this period, would have benefited from these changes and from the protection, in their midst, of one family of greater social importance. In the middle of 15th century there was, in effect, a manor at Little Stoke, but the protection it afforded to the small-holders failed when seriously tested.

The National Archives at Kew holds a fascinating document, written in English some time between 1471 and 1483. It is a petition by Sybil Forster (widow of Robert Poyntz, whose forebears came from Iron Acton, in Gloucestershire) and her husband Humphrey Forster, Esquire, to the then Prince of Wales, Edward Plantagenet, King Edward IV's eldest son. The Forsters held, for a fee, '...*a tenement in Stoke Gyfford other wyse callyd Litill Stoke in the Countie of Glowcester...* '.

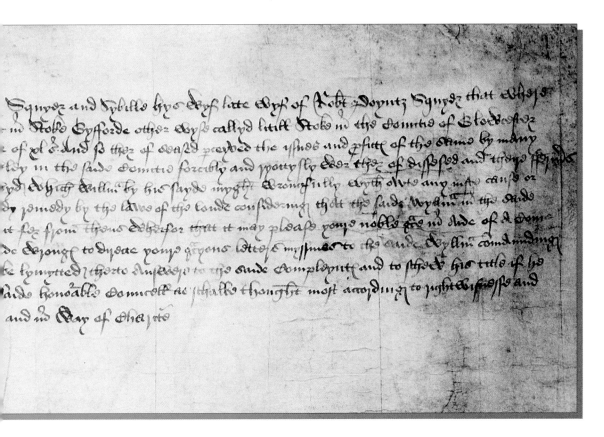

The nature of the petition is summarised, as follows, by the National Archives.

*'The Forsters show that they were for a long time seised of an estate in fee in Stoke Gifford, otherwise called Little Stoke in right of Sybil Forster, and were seised until Berkeley forcibly and riotously disseised them and ousted their farmers and occupiers wrongfully and without any just cause, and still occupies the same, and they can have no speedy remedy by the law of the land considering that Berkeley is of such great might in the county, and the petitioners do not reside in that county. The Forsters request that letters missive be directed to Berkeley commanding him to appear before the prince's council at a certain day to answer the complaints, and to show his title if he has any, and if he fails to do so that further action be directed to be made as is thought right for the speedy relief of the petitioners.'*

The word 'seised' (or seized) is used here to mean 'in legal possession of property and land'. Why they were forcibly evicted may not be known, nor the outcome of the petition. It was made at a turbulent time in English history: Edward, Prince of Wales, became King Edward V at the age of 12, for just a few weeks, before being imprisoned, with his brother Richard, in the Tower of London, by their uncle and

Protector, Richard, Duke of Gloucester. Parliament declared the princes to be illegitimate, enabling the Duke of Gloucester to take the throne as Richard III. The two 'Princes in the Tower' were never seen alive again; presumably murdered. The petition may not have had the outcome that the Forsters would have wished.

'Humphrey Forster, *Squire*' implies that he was a man of social importance, possibly an agent of the Crown, at a politically difficult time. Perhaps as minor gentry, the Forsters had lived for many years in what was an established property at Little Stoke, with surrounding land. Attached were some small-holdings — the document refers to the ousting of the farmers. So, at least 550 years ago, there was a well-established hamlet at Little Stoke.

Coming forwards in time to the 17th century, the land at Little Stoke had been divided into five farmsteads. Tenant farmers came and went. Around 1630 the families tending the land were Grace Grimes, Richard Driner, Israell Holbrow, Mary Bradley and Morris Smith. A 1649 survey shows that two farms were larger than the others; those of Richard Driner and Beth Smyth were 121 and 85 acres, while Thomas Focham, Robert Larence (Lawrence) and Israell Holbrow farmed holdings of 28, 53 and 48 acres respectively. (See also Appendix 3).

A lease document, dated 1665, relating to Little Stoke, has an interesting entry:

*'Also present that Ann Savage widd have one Customary Messuage and 3 Frundells of land for the terme of her life by virtue of the Ct. Roll date 21 April in the 18th Year of King James made by Richard Berkeley to the said Anne…'*

> [Messuage: house, buildings and land; frundell/frandell: ¼ of
> an acre; 18th Year of King James: 1620]

Could this be the origin of the name, Savages Wood, even though the wood was not planted on Little Stoke farmland for another 200 years?

The Gloucestershire Archives hold various wills of the Lawford family, who lived in Stoke Gifford from the late 16th to the early 18th centuries. Thomas Lawford, yeoman, lived at Little Stoke, probably in the most important farmhouse, the older part of the main house that survived into the 1960s. His will is dated 16th May 1690. Although married, Thomas had no surviving children. He leaves the farm and land to his brother's son, also called Thomas — '*I give to my kinsman the son of Robert Lawford aforesaid Thomas Lawford All my Lands lying at Little Stoke aforesaid*

*And my dweling house and all houses dores and gates thereunto belonging to have and to hould to him and his heires for ever'.* If the younger Thomas were to die before the age of 21, the farm at Little Stoke would go to his brother Daniel Lawford, providing he paid his sister, Rachel Lawford, £100 (£7,500 in today's value). Thomas died aged 19, and Daniel, aged 31. The elder Thomas must have been a successful yeoman, leaving the land rights that he owned in Pilning and Siston to other family members. He was born around 1641 and was outlived by both his mother and his wife.

The pattern of five farms was similar in a 1725 survey. The detailed map accompanying this survey shows sketches of the five farmhouses in elevation. The total acreage, around 300, was made up as follows: Mrs Freeman 102, John Harris: 49; Mr Duckenfield: 75; Thomas Baylis: 24, and Samuel Tyson: 54. The Lawfords still had a foothold: Samuel Tyson married Rachel Lawford at Stoke Gifford on the 19th of February 1710. The farms are identified in the survey by the name of the tenant and not by their location on the accompanying map. The map does give the field names then in use, a few of which survived to the 1950s, and the survey lists the fields under each tenant.

*Detail of the 1725 survey map showing the five farms at Little Stoke. Each farm is represented by a sketch of its farmhouse.*

A MAP
OF STOKE GIFFORD
the Seat of
John Berkeley Esq:
with the Mannors of
GREAT STOKE, HARRY STOKE,
and LITTLE STOKE:
Gloucestershire.

By J: Clason.

MDCCXXV.

# North →

A section of the 1725 survey map giving field names in the Little Stoke Manor. The single/ double letters in the fields give the names of the farm tenants: Freeman (F), Duckenfield (D), Harris (H), Baylis (TB) and Tyson (T). Field number 325 (lower right), Fillesses, became Savages Wood in the 1850s. Bradley Stoke Leisure Centre is in Far Fillesses (323). Gipsy Patch Lane meets the A38 at the cross-roads at the upper left of the map, where there is now a modern flyover. A small group of fields, 326, 327, 328, 329, 341 and 342 near the bottom right of the map were part of Tyson's and Freeman's holdings. They were part of the same two farms in 1649. Fields marked with a P were part of John Player's holding at Watch Elm Farm; see pages 40/41.

Crump's land

Ely Chelter's land

Ely Dowel land

Lady Crump land

Ely Chelters land

2 ACRES H

239

251

268 LITTLE BROOKLAND H 258

260 ELMHAY

NEW LEAS H

252 2

264 HOME MEAD 246 35

267

253 GREAT BROOKLAND 255

263

262

PADDOCK 243

265

244 HOME CLOSE 271

UPPER LONG MEAD 255 T

WINSHAY 254 269

Little Stoke

F. 244 HOME CLOSE 271

HOME CLOSE

LITTLE MEAD 256

WINSFURLONG

261

268

270

276

YOUNGMANS

OAT LAND

D 187 CRUNNIS 278

OATLAND 276

277 GREAT DOWN FIELD T

317 MOONS HAMS EAR F

HOMESTEAD D 246

245

279 NEW LEAS T

280 LITTLE DOWN FIELD T

316 MID HAMS EAR F

318 LITTLE FILLESSES AS

Ely Dowel land

283 OAK LEAS TB

281 UPPER DOWN FIELD TB

282 LOWER DOWN FIELD

315 GREAT HAMS EAR F

284 WET LANDS M

319 MID FILLESSES AS

324 GREAT FILLESSES P

MARROW MEAD 286

287 EAR FB

GATNAM FB

288 UPPER GATNAM FB

308 GREAT MATFORD P

UPPER 311 MATFORD P

311 MID MATFORD P

320 GREAT FILLESSES AS

FOOTBRIDG

290

289

GREAT GATNAM FB

306 SUTFIELD FB

309 LITTLE MATFORD P

EAR MATFORD P

313 ELMIN 312

321 HITHER FILLESSES W

322 MID FILLESSES W

EAR FILLESSES W

323

BROOKMEAD P 304

307 BROOKMEAD

BROOK MEAD

310 MATFORD M

MATFORD WT

330 MATFORD W

325 FILLESSES

406

305 ALESBERY B

409 408 407

HALES COMMON

365 DA GREAT RUF

WELSH ACRE MEAD F 336

333 MATFORD F

332 BEAN ACRE P

333 MATFORD CROFT A

329 GREAT MID T

328 LITTLE MATFORD T

327 HOME CRAUGHT F

EAR HOME CRAUGHT F

326

410

401

369 DA HOME GROUND 367

366 DA LITTLE RUF

364 DA WELSH ACRE RB

363

338 MID MATFORD AS

WOOD

334 MATFORD GROUND AS

340 MATFORD LEAS AS

341 LITTLE SANDY CLOSE

342 GREAT SANDY CLOSE T

Tho Perry's land

EAR 360 MATFORD RB

345

GROVE LEAS

LITTLE MEAD

BROAD HAVENS

Which tenant, then, had which farm in 1725? The survey does not make matters clear, although a study of the allocation of fields to each farmer provides some important clues. In addition the survey summary describes Samuel Tyson's Estate as being located *'within the Mannors'* at Little Stoke, whereas the other four farms are described as being *'in Little Stoke besides the commons'*. All five farms lay close to or looked out onto a strip of common land on either side of the modern Clay Lane.

Looking at the field distribution, Mr Harris's farm was the upper farm at the end of the lane (towards the top left in the map on page 11). At the other end of the lane, the small paddock attached to the farmhouse is labelled TB, the farmer there was Thomas Baylis. Opposite is the only farm on the south side of the lane. The fields clustered close by have the letter D, so this would have been Mr Dunkenfield's farm. Samuel and Rachell Tyson's farm was most probably the one next door to the Baylis's farm. This is the most centrally placed of the farms and perhaps this is what *'within the Mannors'* meant. Remember that Rachell Tyson was a beneficiary in Thomas Lawson's will and would have inherited Thomas Lawson's tenancy if her

*1725 Survey: the entry for Samuel Tyson. The three columns of figures give the area of each field in acres (left col.), rods and perches.*
*4 rods = 1 acre,*
*40 perches = 1 rod.*
*(Rods are sometimes called square rods, and perches, square perches).*

*The main entrance to Little Stoke Farm, and the farmhouse, photographed early in 1955. This was the site of Samuel Tyson's farm in 1725 and that of Robert Larance in 1649.*

brother Daniel failed to pay her £100. Thomas, a member of an important wealthy Stoke Gifford family, would have been, in effect, lord of the Little Stoke Manor, but not its owner. The fifth farm then, by elimination, becomes that of Mrs Freeman. Her farmhouse would have been the house at Clay Bottom that survived to the middle of the last century. Her fields, and those of the Tysons, were however, somewhat scattered, but such a pattern was not unusual.

During the next ninety years the number of farms declined. In 1757, there were just three: Thomas Gunter at a single 182 acre farm at Little Stoke, centred on the former farm of Samuel Tyson, with John Sissel (or Sissol) at Harris's Farm, and Mr Cobb, at the farm of his name (previously Mrs Freeman's), both in nearby Clay Bottom. In 1789 Benjamin Dowling held the Little Stoke tenancy, and Edward Gunter that at Clay Bottom, by then a single farm. In 1814 William Willcox, from Butcombe in Somerset, took Little Stoke Farm from the previous tenant, Thomas Hulbert, who had briefly succeeded Benjamin Dowling. Two years later he took over from Edward Gunter. The single 300 acre farm thus formed became the new enlarged Little Stoke Farm. The buildings that made up the other three farms have vanished. The stones from which they were built were probably used in the

*1955: The farm gate is on the left, Tetbury Close now runs through the open gate in the middle. Victor House has replaced the Dutch Barn on the distant right. In 1725 Thomas Baylis's house stood on the site of the cowsheds in the centre of the picture. The barn (left) was part of his farm.*

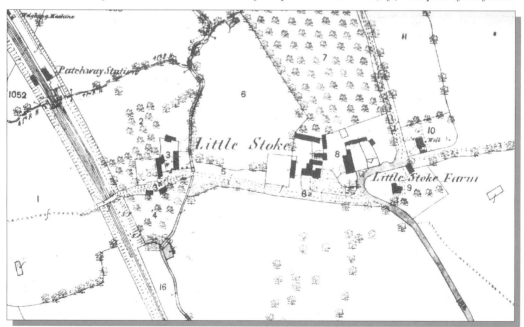

*1881: The site of the original Patchway Station, north of the old bridge which extended Clay Lane over the railway, the only link between the fields separated by the railway. Reproduced from the 1881 Ordnance Survey map.*

*1955: The cottage where Benjamin Weaver and his family lived. To the right of the cottage is the pear tree, here in full bloom, that now stands at the entrance to Clay Lane. Little Stoke Lane curves off to the right towards Stoke Gifford.*

*1955: Four of the farm cottages: on the left the semi-detached red-brick cottages survive to this day, for many years occupied by the Ponting and Cutler families; centre, Rose Dene Cottage home of the Knapp family; right, the home of Bert Williams and his family.*

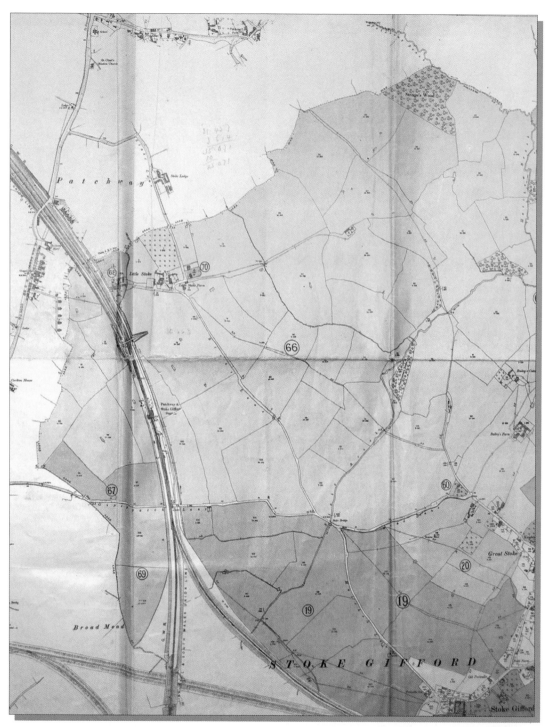

*From the 1915 sale map: The areas labelled 66, 67, 68, 69 and 70 comprised Little Stoke Farm. (The fields to the east of the farm boundary are printed slightly lighter). Savages Wood is near the top right.*

*Benjamin Weaver's cottage in 1930. The stone wall hides Little Stoke Lane from view.*

enlargement of what was to become Little Stoke Farm. William Willcox died in 1819. His widow, Hannah, managed the farm for many years until her death late in 1851. Her son, Benjamin, took over and within a few years the farm grew to 570 acres, the largest of the Stoke Gifford farms by a good margin. He did much to modernise the house and out-buildings (see Appendix 5). The farm that he created was, in essence, the one taken on by my grandfather in 1896.

A survey in 1842 shows that, for a while, Edward Gunter and his wife, Mary, returned to '*a farm at Little Stoke*'. From the fields listed, it must have been John Harris's old farm at Clay Bottom. The Gunters most probably lived in Mr Cobb's adjoining farmhouse. In 1855 their son and daughter, William and Ann, along with a Mr Niblett were living there. However, by 1861, with Benjamin Willcox in charge, the farms were once again united.

\*   \*   \*

So, where exactly was the now vanished small hamlet called Little Stoke? If you walk or drive up Little Stoke Lane from the junction with Gipsy Patch Lane (which runs east from the A38 to Stoke Gifford), passing the Junior and Infant Schools on the right, and the turning into Kingsway and Rossall Avenue on your left, eventually you will come to the junction with Clay Lane. (Let me digress for a moment: Clay Lane is a modern name; in my time at the farm, Little Stoke Lane ran from Gipsy Patch Lane to Station Road. For some reason the last part has been renamed Clay Lane). A magnificent pear tree stands at the junction with Clay Lane with a large new marker stone at its base, on which is mounted an illustrated plaque giving the location of the farm. As you read the inscription you are standing in what was once the highly productive garden of Benjamin Weaver, who worked on the farm for very many years. (The onions that he grew were second to none in size, texture and flavour.) His cottage stood roughly where the first bungalow on your immediate left now stands. Behind you, less than 100 yards distant, was the farmhouse. The farmyards and buildings ran from behind the farmhouse round to the present Victor House. Also just behind you is the entrance to Tetbury Close, and on the far side the first two houses are bungalows. The one on the right stands — perhaps blocks would be the correct word — the former main entrance to the farm. A little further into Tetbury Close, on the left is Morley Close. Less than half way along, the back of the farmhouse is in the front gardens of the houses on the left. In the middle of the road is the dairy, where the milk was cooled before awaiting collection in large churns. On the right, in the front gardens, and I am sorry about this, is a row of three old pigsties!

The hamlet comprised a farm and farmhouse, with five additional cottages. A little further along Clay Lane, down the slight slope, was the other old farmhouse and its outbuildings at Clay Bottom, now Gallivan Close. Before 1816, when it was absorbed into the farm at Little Stoke, this was Cobb's and Harris's Farm, as mentioned earlier. Later the farmhouse was divided and used as three homes for some of the families who worked on the main farm.

When Edward Davis took over Little Stoke Farm in 1896, it was a large farm by local standards: around 560 acres. It extended from the south of Gipsy Patch Lane (west of the railway) up to Savages Wood. To the west its edge was the parish boundary between Stoke Gifford and Patchway. The old Saxon boundary, more than 900 years old, between the Ledbury and Berkeley Hundreds still marked the farm's northern edge. Parts of the hedge along this ancient boundary still exist. And finally, towards Stoke Gifford, Gipsy Patch Lane and Stoke Brook formed most of the rest of the farm's boundary.

During the earlier part of the 20th century it was a dairy farm, growing a range of crops for cattle feed, while a herd of around 60 or more cows were milked twice each day. Up to the mid-1930s, every spring, a flock of sheep regularly produced many lambs. Quite a few pigs were reared, and there is evidence of at least one goat. Ducks, geese and chickens were all free range, laying a regular supply of eggs. Roast goose was at the heart of every Christmas dinner! In the 1940s and 1950s the variety of crops grown was considerable: wheat, oats, barley, potatoes, mangels, swedes and kale. In the summer good crops of hay were mown, mainly for feeding to cattle during the winter.

Surprisingly the land at Little Stoke has been described as 'low grade farm land'. This is an odd description in view of the wide range of crops grown, and the farm's long history. In fact just two stony fields on the north-western edge of the farm were of little use except occasional grazing. However the soil (a Lias clay) was not as rich as that on the alluvial plain closer to the Severn Estuary.

A four-arched bridge, between Clay Lane and Patchway Station, still spans Station Road and the railway lines to and from South Wales. The 'Blue Bridge', as it is

*This photograph was taken from the 'Blue Bridge', looking towards Patchway Station in 1930. An express, probably bound for Cardiff, is just passing through the station. Between the two trees on the left is a glimpse of fields: no Rossall or Lawford Avenues yet. Compare this tranquil scene with the view as it is today (see inset).*

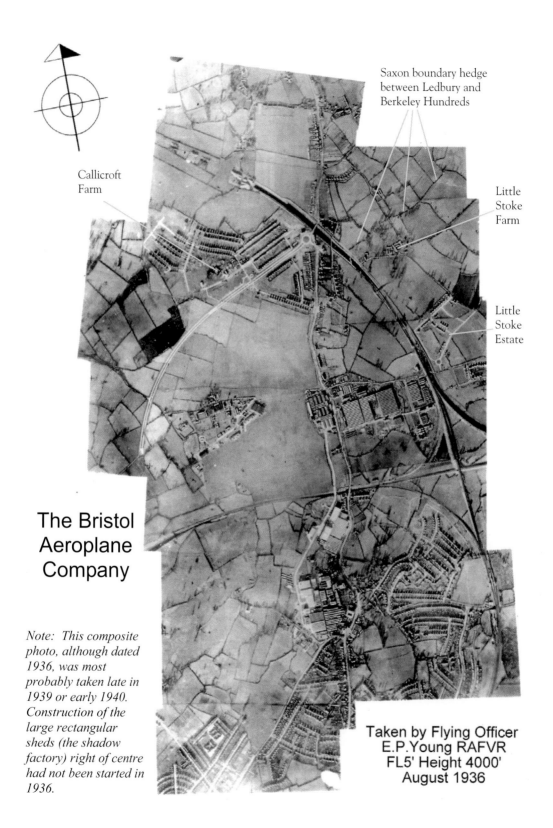

Callicroft
Farm

Saxon boundary hedge
between Ledbury and
Berkeley Hundreds

Little
Stoke
Farm

Little
Stoke
Estate

# The Bristol
# Aeroplane
# Company

*Note: This composite
photo, although dated
1936, was most
probably taken late in
1939 or early 1940.
Construction of the
large rectangular
sheds (the shadow
factory) right of centre
had not been started in
1936.*

Taken by Flying Officer
E.P.Young RAFVR
FL5' Height 4000'
August 1936

often called, was built to join the two parts of the farm, but now serves just as a footbridge. Earlier, when there was only a single railway track, Clay Lane continued over another smaller wooden bridge, long since demolished; the lane reducing to a footpath that ran across a small field that still exists, to the main road through Patchway. The original Patchway Station was just north of this old bridge, but, with the addition of the second lower railway track around 1885, a new station was built, where only a windswept halt now remains. The new station was a real

*Right: The Red Dragon express from South Wales in 1955.*

*Below: The 'Blue Bridge' and Station Road by the junction with Clay Lane in 1953. On the left, Elm trees in their prime. A goods train in the siding allows the express through. The Bristol Aeroplane Company Engine Division buildings are just visible on the right.*

station, with a proper station master, staff, ticket office, waiting rooms and a covered footbridge. Then Station Road joined the A38 at the top end: the people of Patchway were better linked to their station than now! In the 1930s the road and the station, offset by a splendid clump of pine trees, were well maintained.

As the old photograph on page 21 shows, all the land on the far side of the railway was still farmed. Later, during the 1930s and 1940s, this was to change. In the late 1930s Edward Davis sold almost all this part of the farm to the expanding Bristol Aeroplane Company. His son, Howard Davis, continued to farm many of the fields there by arrangement. After the war the Company's Engine Division was built, extending from Gipsy Patch Lane up to and, by the early 1950s, beyond Patchway Station. Later with the break-up of the Aeroplane Company, the Engine Division was taken over by the then Rolls-Royce Ltd, who continue to operate there to this day as Rolls-Royce plc.

In the late 1930s a start was made on the creation of a new Little Stoke, then called Little Stoke Estate, just north of Gipsy Patch Lane. The first houses were built along Rossall Avenue, part of Kingsway and Grange Avenue. These show up clearly on the aerial photograph on page 22. The photograph also includes Callicroft Farm in Patchway just before it was demolished. Also of interest is the airfield in the centre: the runway still had a grass surface!

The tithe map of 1842 gives the names of most of the fields in the parish of Stoke Gifford, names that were more often spoken than written, handed down from one generation to the next. Such names often changed over time, some lasting longer than others. Changes were most likely when a new family took over a farm, or when a field was divided into smaller units, or two fields were combined. Less than half of these names survived to the 1950s, even then with some modifications: Crunnis later became Cronnies ('crow knees'), Oatlands changed slightly to Oaklands, Philips Matford was unchanged for 200 years, Hilly Gatnams was sometimes called Hilly Gatmans, Foot Bridge became Foot Bridges, and Stean Bridge became Stern Bridges by 1896. There are many names that changed out of all recognition: Great Filles's became Top Savages, while Nine Acres and Eight Acres combined to become Lower Savages. Further Filles's became the New (Rough) Ground; Seven Acres and Eleven Acres together, the Old Rough Ground. There were other changes: the lower part of Oatlands became Middle-down; Hither Filles's, Back Cowhouse; Great Mattford, Front Cowhouse; Moorend,

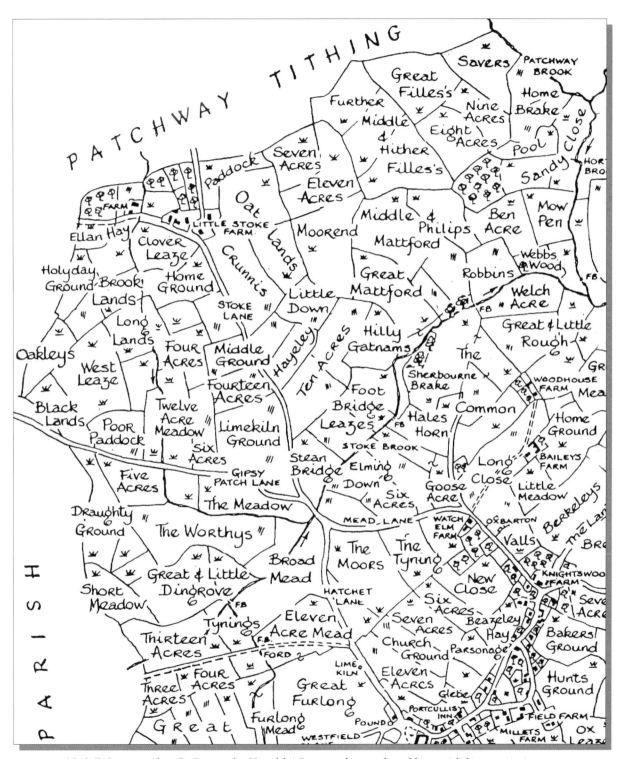

*1842 Tithe map (detail). Drawn by Harold A Lane and reproduced here with his permission.*

*Bailey's Court Farm, farmed in the early 1900s by Edmund Pursey. Photo by Mike Stanbrook.*

Moonies or Moon Hayes — and so on... Savages Wood had not been planted in 1842, the name later being derived either from the field name, Savers, on which the wood was planted, or after a family that lived at Little Stoke over 200 years earlier.

Do any of these names have a place in the new town of Bradley Stoke? Sadly, the answer is 'only a few'; but on the land that was once Little Stoke Farm, none! Looking at a street map of the area, it is clear that the planners and builders may have overlooked the opportunity to make good use of many of these old names, to forge a link between the new and what had gone before. There is, of course, one exception: Savages Wood Road. Sometimes the names sow confusion: one roundabout on Savages Wood Road, although on the former Little Stoke Farm, is called Manor Farm! (Manor Farm, before it, too, vanished, was further north at Patchway Common). An opportunity does, however, exist for some house owners to adopt the old field names for their homes, to celebrate and mark the history of the area and its landscape. A few field names have been used to name roads elsewhere. On land that was once part of Bailey's Court Farm, near Stoke Brook, but on the wrong side, is Stean Bridge Road; Sherbourne Avenue is well placed near the Brake of the same name, but The Crunnis is nowhere near the original field by Bert William's cottage at Little Stoke; while Limekiln Gardens is far to the north of its origin by Gipsy Patch Lane!

\* \* \* \* \*

# Chapter 2

# Bradley Stoke

A chapter about Bradley Stoke 50 and more years ago — now that's a curious idea! Little Stoke Farm, Bailey's Court, Bowsland Farm and the area around Patchway Common were all still part of rural south Gloucestershire. The names Bradley and Stoke had yet to be prised out of the beds of two local streams and conjoined.

House-building at the new Bradley Stoke started in the early 1980s, more as a large housing development than a carefully planned and integrated township. It grew rapidly, initially without a clear sense of its own identity, and in its early 'teenage years', suffered in the recession of the 1990s. The press unkindly wrote of 'Sadly Broke' and, perhaps even more unkindly, of 'the negative equity capital of Europe'. Growth was on hold but as the economic outlook improved so did the fortunes of Bradley Stoke. It gained in confidence as its administration moved from that of a Parish to a Town Council. Recently a new town centre has been built close to Savages Wood. Tesco has opened a new larger superstore there to replace their previous one. Bradley Stoke Community School is now well established in its new premises close to the wood. There is a library, churches, doctors' surgeries and a few pubs: its identity is evolving.

What did the landscape look like before all this came about? The photograph at the top of the next two pages provides the answer. It is a hot August day in 1955. The corn is being cut in Top Savages, using an old binder pulled by a tractor, while the neat string-bound sheaves of cut corn are arranged in stooks to dry out. Savages Wood provides an appropriate backdrop to this idyllic harvest-time activity.

How, then, is this scene different now? Savages Wood still stands, its trees aging, with Bradley Stoke Way running across, close to the wood's edge. The earlier, now demolished, Tesco superstore was once just left of centre and is now the car park for its replacement. The newly finished town centre is at the far right of the photograph.

*1955: Harvesting at what is now Bradley Stoke town centre. Savages Wood lies beyond (see p31).*

If you look at a modern street map of Bradley Stoke and Little Stoke an odd feature emerges. I will illustrate this with the route taken, in 1955, by a load of wheat from the scene in the above photograph to the farm. The field names are those in use then. After leaving Top Savages the load heads due south across Back Cowhouse, passing through a gate by a clump of trees, where hay and straw ricks were often built and thatched. On then into Front Cowhouse, past the low stone cowsheds and walled pens that gave the fields their names. The direction now swings almost

due west along a stony track that led straight to the farm. Next the load hugs the northern edge of Moon Hayes (or Moonies: I never saw it written down). Down into a dip, the tractor and its load crosses the stream that runs now by Braydon Avenue, and then along the track that crosses Oaklands, before emerging between Rose Dene Cottage and the house where the Williams family lived. The entrance to the farm is just a few yards along the lane. The load has arrived at its destination.

Could I take the empty wagon back for another load today, even if it was waiting? The answer is an emphatic No! The track between the two houses has vanished

1. Load emerging into Front Cowhouse.

2. The sheds and ricks in Front Cowhouse.

4. Load crossing Oaklands; Savages Wood in the distance.

3. Crossing Moon Hayes.

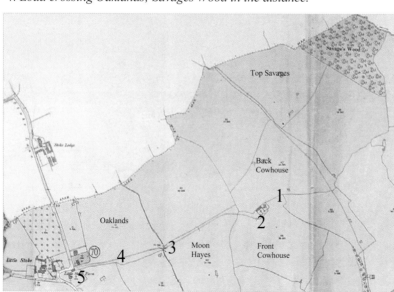

5. Arriving at the farm by Bert William's and Rose Dene cottages.

*Left: The journey from Top Savages to the farm. The numbers refer to the photographs above.*

and new homes have been built there, but that is not the important feature. On the far side of what had been Oaklands lies Braydon Avenue. It accompanies an attractive hedge and stream-side walk down to Stoke Brook. There are many places where walkers can cross the stream. But for anyone in a car, Braydon Way is a barrier, albeit invisible, but all too real for the driver, between modern Little Stoke and its larger Bradley Stoke sibling. The poor driver has to venture down to the end of Braydon Avenue by Stoke Brook, or make his or her way via the roundabout on the A38, by Aztec West. Why divide the communities in this way?

But wait a moment: the hedge and stream beside Braydon Avenue is the old Saxon boundary between the two large open fields that once extended from the Little Stoke hamlet to and beyond the modern Savages Wood. The first field, called Down, reached all the way to the centre of Great Stoke. It is remarkable that so much of this boundary has survived unbroken into the present. At its northern end it met the line of another Saxon hedge, parts of which still grow. (See Appendix 1)

From the new town centre, Savages Wood Road starts encouragingly as it heads towards the site of the farm; but after the roundabout on Brook Way, it loses its sense of purpose, soon becoming a footpath before reaching the bend in Braydon Avenue. (I remember an oak tree and a small pond at the corner of the field there). Perhaps there are plans ... I would like to collect that second load!

*   *   *   *   *

*June 29th 2009: The 'harvest scene' shown across pages 28 and 29, as it is today.*

*Edward Henry Kempton Davis, 1875-1957. Photographed in 1949.*

*Howard Henry Davis, 1898-1974. Photographed in 1964.*

# Chapter 3

# Family Connections

It was over 50 years ago in late summer of 1958 that my parents, Howard and Mabel Davis, locked the front door of the farmhouse at Little Stoke for the last time and left. I was 21 years old then, the start of adulthood in those times, and away studying at college in London. Curiously, I have little recollection of the move to the new family home in Clapton in Gordano, in Somerset. However my memories, though far from complete, are of the wonderful years growing up on the farm. It is hard to imagine a better place to gain an understanding of life, nature and the seasons, than on such a farm. There was always something new to discover, to learn about and to understand. Life was not without its dangers, and the warnings were duly heeded. While ducks and chickens were quite safe, geese, particularly the ganders, could be quite vicious if approached closely; to get between a cow and its calf was decidedly dangerous, while bulls could be, and often were, bad-tempered – best viewed at a distance, from the other side of a stout fence — and wasps had an end that dispensed a particularly nasty sting. These lessons were learned early, without mishap (except for the wasps, that is).

Of course it was not all a matter of preserving life and limb. Haymaking and harvest were times that cast their own magic spells: the smell of new mown hay; the swaying of ripening barley as a light breeze swept across the growing field. There was the wonder of Savages Wood at the top end of the farm: few outsiders trod its paths then. Under my father's stewardship it was managed as a wildlife refuge. Closer to home, in the main yard at the farm, was the barn, long since demolished. In today's times it would have been preserved, perhaps converted into a luxury home. Then it was where the winter cattle food was produced — belts from wheels along an axle that extended from the front of the barn to the back, gave life to machines to chop straw into chaff, to slice mangels and other root crops, and grind corn into flour. The mixture was fed to the milking cows in their stalls in winter months, when the ground was too wet and the grass too short for grazing. Until the

1950s all cows were milked by hand, twice a day. Milking machines were then installed, which was not to the liking of every cow! All these things helped to make it a rich and rewarding childhood. So it ended in 1958; this dream-like existence, as well as the family links with the farm, sometimes complicated, that extended back over the centuries.

*L to R: William Cutler, Thomas Cook and Harry Ponting, some time in the 1920s. (J. Thawley)*

Edward Davis became the full owner of Little Stoke Farm when, in 1915, the Badminton Estate auctioned all the land and dwellings that it owned in Stoke Gifford, which was practically the whole village and surrounding lands. He bought the farm, the farm cottages and a few additional adjoining fields, around 560 acres in total, for £10,000.

There were others whose lives were interwoven with the running of the farm. Their families lived in the cottages that were attached to the farm, including the former farmhouse at Clay Bottom. The list of names may not be complete, as memories after 50 years can be less than sharp. There was Thomas Cook, Benjamin Weaver, Harry Ponting, William Cutler, Bert Williams, Jim Wyatt, Stan Richens, John Cook and all their families. Victor Knapp and his family lived at Rose Dene cottage; he worked at the aeroplane company. If there were others, who have slipped my memory, I apologise, for I would have wished to include them here. Perhaps their descendants will recognise their faces when they read this book.

*1930s: Coldharbour Farmhouse.*

So, winding the clock back in stages… Edward Henry Kempton Davis, my grandfather, took over tenancy of Little Stoke Farm in 1896: the start of a chain of events that included the birth of my father, Howard Davis, in 1898; his marriage, in 1931, at St Michael's Church, Stoke Gifford, to Mabel Pierce of Coldharbour Farm (on the south side of Stoke Gifford) and my own birth in 1937. Although the Second World War was declared before I had reached the grand age of two years, its effect had little impact on me that I was able to understand.

*Above: The marriage of Howard Davis and Mabel Pierce at St Michael's Church, Stoke Gifford, 2nd June, 1931. An archway of rakes and pitchforks was provided by the men who worked on the farm at Little Stoke. Harry Ponting is third from the left (with his unmistakable moustache), and William Cutler is third from the right.*

*Left: Mabel Pierce, of Church Farm, Filton, and later, Coldharbour Farm, Stoke Gifford, at the age of 21.*

As I will describe in more detail later, the nearby railway and Bristol Aeroplane Company on the far side of the tracks attracted the attention of the Luftwaffe in 1940. During this period I was packed off to Wotton-under-Edge in Gloucestershire for safety, and my parents resolved not to travel anywhere together. An Anderson air-raid shelter was erected in one downstairs room in the farmhouse, surrounded, again for safety, by hundreds of sand-filled bags. The bombs, when they came, did not, therefore, affect my happy childhood memories of growing up on the farm, memories that I still treasure.

Edward's father, Henry Davis of Leigh Farm, near Pensford, just south of Bristol, was born in 1836 at Callicroft Farm, the home of Edward (senior) and Ann Davis, in what is now Patchway. Then it was part of the parish of Almondsbury, in Gloucestershire. None of the buildings of Callicroft Farm has survived. It was approached by a track from the A38 that ran a few yards north, and parallel to the present Callicroft Road. The farm entrance was at the top of the track, just where the main doors lead one into the Patchway Community Centre (or as it was known in my younger days, The Social Hall). My mother was heavily involved with the Patchway Gardens Guild in the immediate post-war years, and I have lasting memories of the Flower Shows at that echoing Social Hall.

My family connections to Little Stoke Farm stretch back, in a roundabout way, at least 200 years, if not much further. Edward Davis senior, Henry's father, died

*Above: Callicroft Farm, c1910. Top right, Edward Davis Snr. Bottom right, Henry Davis in 1860.*

before Henry was two years old. A year later Edward's widow and cousin, Ann, married Joseph Willcox of Stoke Gifford and they continued to farm at Callicroft. Over the next few years Henry had acquired a total of seven brothers and sisters. In this story one sister is important: Emma Willcox, born in 1847 at Callicroft. Joseph had an older sister Mary who had married Richard Bennett Witchell. They lived at Field Farm in Stoke Gifford and their oldest son Sidney Witchell married his cousin, the afore-mentioned Emma Willcox in the spring of 1881. They farmed another great Stoke Gifford farm, Bailey's Court, before taking over Little Stoke Farm in 1886. Sidney Witchell died in 1895. The stage was then set for my grandfather, Edward, to take over from Emma, his aunt, in 1896. Between 1853 and 1886 Benjamin Willcox, Joseph's brother, farmed at Little Stoke.

Joseph's father was William Willcox of Butcombe in Somerset. He and his wife, Hannah, and their children moved to Stoke Gifford and in 1814 took over Little Stoke Farm from the previous tenant, Thomas Hulbert. William kept a detailed, somewhat randomly organised account book of all his transactions. This account book, dated 1799, survives to the present day, and it makes interesting, if amusing reading. Two extracts have been included here.

*Benjamin Willcox of Little Stoke Farm from 1853 to 1886.*

*Above: Emma Willcox of Callicroft Farm married Sidney Witchell in 1881. They farmed at Little Stoke from 1886.*

*Left: Field Farm, Stoke Gifford, in 1881. Three ladies of the Witchell family: centre is Susan Witchell, one of the other older women is her mother, Mary Witchell, née Willcox, sister of Joseph and Benjamin Willcox, born around 1800.*

The accounts were randomly organised in that William seems to have opened the book and written on whatever page lay before him; sometimes working from the front, at others from the back — tracking a sequence in time can be a challenge. His spelling was, to say the least, independent!

Thomas Hulbert was paid 15 pounds and six shillings for items that lay outside the tenancy terms of the Beaufort Estate: *To paid for Ston Grat in the parler — 0 . 10 0* (10 shillings) and so on.

*Extract from William Willcox's accounts when he took over Little Stoke Farm in 1814.*

A little further down what is now Clay Lane, close to the present railway line to South Wales, lay the smaller Cobb's and Harris's Farm, by then a single farm, later known as Clay Bottom. In 1816 William Willcox took over the tenancy from Edward Gunter, paying him the then considerable sum of 226 pounds and 10 shillings (about £6,800 today) for the stock, live and dead, on the farm. From then on Cobb's and Harris's became an integral part of Little Stoke Farm. William died in 1819, and it was his widow, Hannah who continued to manage the farm, until her death in 1852. She became known as 'Widow Willcox'.

In William and Hannah's time the farm covered only 300 acres. Widow Willcox appears to have run the farm successfully for some 34 years. It would have

1816

A Count of the Stock as I Bought for the
Farm of Gunters

| | | £ | s | d |
|---|---|---|---|---|
| April 29 | To 1 3 years ould haiffer | 10 | 0 | 0 |
| may 2 | ~~...~~ haiffer 8.8.0 | 17 | 3 | 0 |
| Do 8 | To 1 2 years ould haiffer 8.15.0 To 1 3 years ould | | | |
| | To 1 2 years ould haiffer 8.8.0 To 1 3 Do ould haiffer | 16 | 17 | 0 |
| Do 13 | To 1 3 years ould haiffer | 11 | 0 | 0 |
| Do | To 1 3 years ould haiffer | 9 | 0 | 0 |
| Do | To 1 Cone 9..0..0 2 yearlings haiffers 6..12.6 | 15 | 12 | 6 |
| Do | To 1 Plough 1.15.0 Do 1..9..0 Do 2.0.6 | 2 | 16 | 6 |
| Do | To 1 pair Drags 1.0.0 Do 1..0..0 Do Drags 1..9.0 | 3 | 9 | 0 |
| Do | To Shaft for Roller 13 Pigs 3.17.0 | 4 | 10 | 0 |
| Do | To Scorn Screen 1..6.0 & Whin fan 3..5.. | 1 | 11 | 6 |
| Do 16 | To 2 3 years ould haiffers 14..0.0 & 1 2 years ould haiffer | 21 | 0 | 0 |
| Do | To 14 team Wethers Sheep | 17 | 10 | 0 |
| Do 23 | To 2 3 years ould haiffers 13..12.6 | 13 | 12 | 6 |
| Do 30 | To 2 3 years ould haiffers 21..0. & 1 3 years ould | 28 | 0 | 0 |
| June 6 | To 1 2 years ould haiffer | 8 | 12 | 0 |
| Do 20 | To 1 3 years ould haiffer | 10 | 18 | 0 |
| July 20 | To 1 Bull | 7 | 17 | 0 |
| Sept 1 | To 6 3 years ould Steers | 30 | 0 | 0 |
| | | £226 | 10 | 0 |
| 1814 march 25 | A Count of all the Stock as I Bought and all the Expence as I was at | 165 | 2 | 0 |
| | | 391 | 12 | 0 |

*Extract from William Willcox accounts when he took over Cobb's and Harris's Farm in 1816.*

primarily been a dairy farm. The Bristol Mercury, on 12th March 1853, gave notice of the sale following her death. The livestock comprised 63 cattle, 235 sheep, cart and nag horses, and store pigs. Deadstock: ten ricks of wheat and oats, six mows of hay, about 100 tons of roots, complete sets of farming implements, dairy and brewing utensils, and an apple mill and press.

In 1842 a Surveyor and Land Agent produced a report on the Stoke Gifford Farms. It concluded that many of them were poorly managed, run down and much in need of improvement. There were exceptions: Court Farm and Little Stoke Farm were commended: Hannah Willcox had discharged her responsibilities well!

On her death her son Benjamin Willcox continued to run the farm with the help of his sister, also Hannah. In the 1861 census its size is given as 570 acres, and it remained so until Edward Davis sold some land for development in the 1930s. Savages Wood was most probably planted at the top end of the farm shortly after Benjamin took over.

There is an earlier family link to the farm, even more convoluted to follow, possibly as far back as the mid 1680s. It is a distant relationship, one involving marriages and distant cousins; but it is a link, nevertheless. In the mid-1700s John Player, a member of a local Quaker family, lived at Watch Elm Farm, on the northern edge of Great Stoke, as had his father, Jacob and grandfather, John. Just opposite the farmhouse stood the remarkable stump of an enormous elm tree, where those whose duty it was to keep a protective watch on the village would meet. So taken was the observant John Player that he sketched and described this magnificent stump in these words:

*'I have also made a homely Drawing of the old Elm Tree at Stoke which stands Opposite my fore door On the Comon [it gave the farm its name, Watch Elm Farm.] Tis doubtless very Ancient I cannot learn how Old. It has been Called the Watch Elm for Upwards of 80 years and was before that time a Lodging place for hogs; it At that time being to appearance very Ancient and much Dismemberd this is Verified by one Sarah Hibbs now Living Aged 96 whose memory is strong and quick and has dwelt in this Parrish most of her time. It was called the Watch Elm from its being the place where in former times those who were appointed to do watch and ward did meet to go their Respective Rounds from'.*

*Watch Elm Farm buildings, photographed in 1956. The farmhouse once stood in the foreground.*

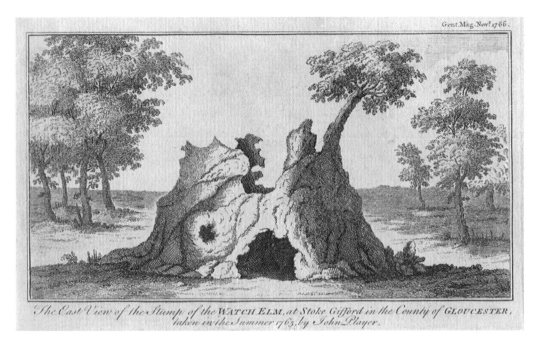

*The East View of the Stump of the WATCH ELM, at Stoke Gifford in the County of GLOUCESTER, taken in the Summer 1765, by John Player.*

*1776: The stump of the Stoke Gifford Watch Elm, sketched by John Player.*

He also wrote about the tree in an article in the November 1766 edition of the *Gentlemen's Magazine*. Although Watch Elm farmhouse was demolished in mid-Victorian times, the farm buildings survived into the second half of the 20th century, before they, too, were demolished to make way for the expansion of Stoke Gifford. At the time John Player farmed there, the land was divided up very differently between the Stoke Gifford farms.

Watch Elm was a mixed farm, which then included a number of fields close to the future Savages Wood that later became part of Little Stoke Farm. However John Player did more than just farm: he was also a surveyor and a grain merchant. His main crops were wheat and barley; but he also grew turnips, beans and peas, the latter probably as a fallow crop to rejuvenate the soil. He kept cattle, sheep and pigs. When he left the farm, his livestock numbered 40 cattle. The pattern of farming was not significantly different from that 200 years later, the main changes being in the technology of farm implements: seed drills, mowers, binders, threshing machines, etc.

John Player had a brother, Jacob. A great great grand child of this Jacob later married Mary Davis, who was a cousin of Edward Davis of Callicroft Farm. Both Mary's father, John Davis, and Edward's father, William Davis were brothers, born at Clapton Court in Clapton in Gordano. As I said, a very convoluted connection!

Robert Poyntz was mentioned briefly in Chapter 1, together with his widow, Sybil. She was his second wife, his first wife being Jane. Robert's line stretches back nine generations to Hugh Poyntz, born sometime in the mid-1100s. Robert's great-great-grandfather, Sir Nicholas Poyntz, was Sheriff of Gloucestershire in 1363, and his grandfather was Sir Robert Poyntz of Iron Acton. One of Sir Robert's later descendants married a Player, who was a distant relative of the above mentioned Jacob. So I have a family connection, by marriage, with Little Stoke of some 540 years! But, in fairness, I probably have some sort of link with dozens of farms all over south Gloucestershire: farmers' sons usually married other farmers' daughters.

Meanwhile, what happened to the farm at Little Stoke? Chipping Sodbury Rural District Council had purchased it from the Davis family in 1957 — for just £30,000! For a brief spell my parents became their tenants. After 1958 Markham Gay and his family took over the tenancy of the farm and some of the land for a few years. But by the late 1960s the farmhouse and buildings stood empty, unloved and unused. A public meeting was held to decide its future, but nothing came of it.

*The farmhouse in 1892, with a Willcox family group: the darkly dressed woman at the centre is Emma Willcox. In front are her two children: Richard (left, in a pram) and Mary. The woman on the left, holding the pram, has not been identified.*

Soon decay set in, the house was broken into and vandalised. The Rural District Council seemed to take little action to prevent this process, or to find a new use for the buildings. I paid a visit at the time. Walking in through the wide-open front door, a sad sight met me; the banisters lay broken and it was dangerous to walk upstairs. I did, and the familiar rooms were all there, but derelict; the overcast sky visible through a hole in the roof. In the large farmhouse kitchen the old AGA cooker had been wrenched from its base and lay face down on the floor. Outside, the garden was overgrown, the green door at the end, that led into the main yard, was missing. Through the opening I could see the barn, its roof starting to sag, as it became an increasing danger to anyone who entered. The inevitable happened, everything, bar the two red brick semi-detached cottages, built in 1908, was levelled to make way for new houses. All that now remains of the farm are those two cottages, an apple tree and a pear tree, both once part of the old orchard - and the other pear tree that stood erect in Benjamin Weaver's cottage garden. It now stands, still erect and somewhat larger, at the junction of Clay Lane and Little Stoke Lane, a glorious sight when in full bloom, commemorating, with a plaque, what has long since disappeared, And it still stands there only because years ago some local residents won a hard fought campaign for its preservation.

Needless to say, I did not return for many years, not until almost every sign of what had once been Little Stoke, had completely vanished. Fortunately my parents and

*All that remains of the farm: the two semidetached red brick cottages, built in 1908 and on the right, Benjamin Weaver's pear tree. A plaque, placed in 2008, marks the farm's location.*

grandparents left behind over 400 hundred photographs. Many of these are shared with you in this book.

\*　　\*　　\*

So when the door was finally locked at Little Stoke Farm on that late summer day in 1958, Howard Davis was returning to the place of one of his ancestral roots, Clapton in Gordano — and leaving another. The wheel had turned full circle!

\*　\*　\*　\*　\*

*1918: Three Davis generations. Seated: Henry; standing: right, Edward; left, Howard.*

# Chapter 4
# Little Stoke Farm:
## the house, yards and garden

*The farmhouse in 1890, a few years after the part to the right of the porch had been rebuilt. Parts of the rest date back to the 17th Century, or even earlier.*

The house at Little Stoke was a typical farmhouse of its time. Parts were late Victorian, others much earlier. It had a large kitchen, with a big central wooden table standing on an uneven flagstone floor. This was later covered with layers of newspaper to smooth out the uneven bumps, with an added, lightly coloured, linoleum overlay. Within my time the original range was replaced by a cream coal-fired AGA cooker. An early model refrigerator stood in one corner and a tall upright water softener in another, by the sink. It was in an age before the universal fitted kitchen: there was a work surface and shelving, both dark green, along one side and plenty of deep cupboard space either side of the AGA.

Next to the kitchen was the even larger dining room, facing the front garden on two sides. Its solid oak floor was said to have come from trees felled on the farm: the boards tightly packed and hard-wearing. In the centre of the room was a large dining room table; too large for most modern houses. It would easily seat eight without the extension pieces. There was a sofa by the front window, and in the corner a black shiny grand piano. Signed prints of birds by the artist, Archibald Thorburn, hung on the walls. They were my father's choice: he was an ornithologist.

Also downstairs was a tiled hall (fitted carpets can get dirty too quickly in a farmhouse), a long narrow scullery that led to an apple storeroom, a study that was lined with my father's ever growing library of bird books, and, at the end of the

*1940s: The hallway, with its tiled floor and staircase at Little Stoke.*

*Above: The early shoots of creeper had, between 1890 and 1908 covered the newer part of the farmhouse. Standing by the house are Edward Davis, his wife and two of their daughters.*

passageway, a drawing room, to which the family would withdraw in comfort after a hearty meal. Now it would be called the lounge. Some of the furniture and pictures from that room surround me reassuringly, as I write. Perhaps, long ago, Thomas Lawford entertained visitors by candle-light, and on cold winter evenings, a roaring log fire, in this same room in the 1680s.

There were five bedrooms upstairs; three were large and all could house a double bed. A bathroom had been added upstairs as an afterthought. It was cramped, but did provide useful cover for someone below, waiting just outside the backdoor.

The toilet, next to the bathroom, was unusual and fully deserves its own paragraph. It had a large hinged mahogany seat that extended from wall to wall. However, it was the flush that was remarkable. Above the toilet, a large water tank was set into the roof, about five or six feet square and at least three or four feet deep. Gutters channelled rain-water into its welcoming arms. Small aquatic creatures grew and flourished in its depths. In one corner was a plug and a lever to raise and lower it, operated by the chain that hung down in the room below. To use the flush, the chain had to be pulled and held. An almighty rush of water, including small water-boatmen and other tiny creatures, unwisely caught too close to the plug, rapidly and vigorously cleared the toilet bowl in couple of seconds. Visitors were baffled: the normal pull and quick release, achieved little. The trick was not to hand out any instructions! Long summer droughts, however, produced their own problems...

There were three other rooms — more farm than farmhouse, and mainly used for storage. Outside the backdoor was a small, rather dour, flag-stoned courtyard, partly sheltered by a sloping roof. Under it, one flag-stone bore a large **W** carved deep into its coarse surface, marking the stone-walled well beneath that once supplied the farmhouse with water. Beyond this was the dairy where the milk was cooled as it filled the churns. A large adjoining washroom served to keep the milk pails spotlessly clean after each round of milking.

The farm was divided into a main yard between the house and barn, along with three others, each with cowsheds that provided enough winter accommodation for the cattle. There was one small Dutch barn in the main yard, and two others in the rick yard. An aging orchard lay beyond the main yard, mostly with apple and a few pear trees. Each autumn the hedge at the far end produced a heavy crop of tasty blackberries.

There were two ponds attached to the yards, neither being quite what it seemed. They did provide cattle with somewhat muddy drinking water; although there were drinking troughs for the cows, with good clean water. One pond, the smaller of the two, was close to the main farm gate. It tended to silt up all too quickly. When cleared, a cobbled stone floor was exposed, sloping steeply towards the back of the pond, hardly a good foothold for cows when drinking. I learned later that the pond was for maintaining carts, although I never witnessed it being used in this way.

Victorian cart wheels were made of wood; different types for different parts, chosen for their particular properties. A hot iron rim or tyre was fitted to complete each wheel. As the iron cooled it gripped the wheel tightly. With use, joints in the wheel, and the tyre, itself, would loosen. A horse would then back the cart down the cobbled slop, immersing its wheels. Water was absorbed, the wood expanded, making both joints and rim tight. Problem solved.

The little pond was only big enough for a two wheeled cart: what about those with four? I remember something I had seen in the other larger pond, which lay to the right of the small Dutch barn in the main yard. The pond faced into the orchard. Originally its front edge was a line of tightly laid flat stones (see photo below), in line with the orchard wall. By my childhood these had vanished, or had been submerged. Gradually the pond became extended, arcing out into the orchard. It too became silted over the years; and only once, in my recollection, was it cleaned out, exposing the sloping cobbled base, this time extending much further back.

*1922: Edward Davis' daughter, Hilda, watches the geese from the flagstones on the edge of the orchard pond. To the right of her, its trunk partly obscured by her arm, is a pear tree. Remarkably this pear tree survives, now in a front garden off Tetbury Close (right).*

Each side of the central hollow, which was wide enough for a wagon, were two paved walkways, like narrow platforms at a station. The walkways had become submerged with time. This then is where the four wheeled wagons had their wheels tightened; the walkways giving easy access for maintenance.

Finally the front garden, my mother's pride and joy, was large, extending out from two sides of the house. It was at its best in the late 1940s and early 1950s, particularly when the wonderful beds of irises were in full bloom.

*1922: Orchard Pond. Edward's daughter, Christine, feeding the ducks, which are swimming in the deep part where cart wheels were once immersed. The submerged walkway can just be seen to their right.*

Photographs, not words, do the garden a greater justice, as some that follow later in this chapter will show...

*1956: The front garden in summer.*

*1908: Cattle in the home field, in front of the house and farm buildings.*

*Little Stoke farmhouse in 1930 — little had changed externally.*

*Early 1920s:  Entertaining on the front lawn. Note the wind-up gramophone by the summerhouse.*

*1920: A young Howard Davis trying out a Singer sports car in the main yard.  The barn is on the left. A new Dutch barn stands behind the car and the orchard lies beyond.*

*Around 1930, repairs were needed to the main chimney. This gave an opportunity to photograph the farm buildings from a good vantage point. Top right is the view looking north west towards Patchway. One or two buildings along the A38 can just be seen between the trees. The field beyond the buildings and wall was named the Home Close. The white dots by the hedge on the right are geese. The lower picture shows the main yard looking north east. Howard Davis stands facing the camera. Benjamin Weaver pushes a wheelbarrow. Victor House now stands on the site of the middle Dutch barn. Two apple trees in the orchard can just be seen between and beyond the Dutch barns. Five magnificent Elm trees form the backdrop — a common tree in south Gloucestershire before their wholesale destruction by the Dutch elm disease beetle.*

The above picture shows the main farm entrance looking south east. Benjamin Weaver's cottage is on the far side of Little Stoke Lane. Most of this large cottage garden was used to grow vegetables. The horse stands just outside the stables that formed part of the barn. A ladder leads to a hayloft, from which hay could be fed down to the horses. At the time horses provided the only means of traction. The man holding the horse has not been identified.

The lower photograph shows the view to the south west. A green-house stands in the corner of the large walled kitchen garden. This kitchen garden, with its magnificent Victoria plum tree, is just beyond the wide second farm entrance. The lane to the right runs to Clay Bottom and Station Road. Straight ahead, beyond the railway line are open fields. The faint outline of houses along the A38 can just be seen. More elm trees line the lane on the right.

*Clay Bottom in 1950. This old house, once Cobb's and Harris's Farm, became part of Little Stoke Farm in 1816. It lacked all services in the first half of the 20th century. Water was drawn from a well in the front courtyard. Thomas Cook and family lived at the right hand end, and cooked using an old two chimney paraffin stove. The Richens family lived briefly during the 1950s in the middle section. Jim Wyatt and his wife Betty moved into the left hand part in 1947.*

*The trees on the left and right survive and the old gateway is now the entrance to Gallivan Close.*

*Ann Richens drawing water from the well at Clay Bottom.*

*Benjamin Weaver and cat at his cottage gate in the early 1950s.*

*Right: the approach to Little Stoke along Little Stoke Lane in 1955 — Ben Weaver's pear tree in full bloom is just right of centre.  Left:  the same tree in May 2008, once again in full bloom.*

*The farmhouse on a spring day in the early 1950s. The ivy had been removed because of damage to the mortar. The small windows under the eaves let light into the attic in the older part of the house. Lines in the stonework at the end of the house (top left) show that at some time the roof had been raised, probably to fit the attic windows.*

*Below and right: The main farm entrance from outside the gate (below), and the view from within, in the opposite direction (right).*

*Above: The second farm entrance in the 1950s. The gate is the same as in the photograph opposite.*
*Below: The main farm entrance in the spring in 1954, with magnolia in full bloom.*

*1954: View from the front door towards the majestic elm trees in the front field.*

In the 1950s the garden at the farm was at its best.  A wide bed of irises extended the full length of the front of the house.  There was an old green door, hidden from view here, that gave access to the main yard. It had to be kept shut: once cattle did get through, doing untold damage. The large kitchen garden produced plums apples and many vegetables.  It also housed a few beehives.  The bees had plenty of flowers from which to make their honey, which, in most years, was sold to passers by.

*Around 1950: More front garden scenes showing the irises in full bloom. In the top photo the old cider press from Clay Bottom serves as a garden feature, surrounded by plants.*

*1950: An unusual view of the house and lawn from the dell. This last part of the garden, squeezed in by the main farm gate, contained a small group trees, small flower beds and narrow stone paths. We called it 'The Dell'.*

\* \* \* \* \*

*1954: A view towards the rick yard, over the ice-covered orchard pond. On the left, a Dutch barn; on the right, partly obscured, is Rose Dene Cottage.*

# Chapter 5

# Livestock

Before the outbreak of the Second World War the horse was king, as it had been for centuries. Without horses, arable farming would not have been possible. The huge carthorses were used for all forms of traction. Either singly, in pairs, or in teams, they pulled everything: ploughs to turn the soil, harrows and rollers to break and prepare it for sowing, drills to sow the seeds, grass cutters to mow the hay and, at harvest time, the binder to reap and tie the standing corn into sheaves — and this is only some of their uses. They always appeared to me as docile, good-natured willing beasts, which, in expert hands, seemed able to anticipate all that was expected of them. Sometimes, when not working, they enjoyed the freedom of an open field. The sight of a large cantering horses was inspiring but when at full gallop, perhaps frightening, as they made the ground shake! At other times they were housed in their stable quarters at the end of the barn, by the main entrance gate. Each horse had its own stall and manger into which food was dropped from the hayloft above. Old leather harnesses, with tarnished brass buckles, hung from large aging grey wooden pegs on the dusty whitewashed wall behind the magnificent beasts. It could have looked the same at any time during the last three hundred years or more. If history has a smell, this was full of it! Just beyond the last stall, a short passage on the left led to two small musty storage rooms, one with a chute to the chaff cutter above in the main part of the barn. The horses were well cared for: they were important!

*About 1925: Foal and its mother.*

*1955: 'Blossom', the last horse at Little Stoke.*

# Horses at work during haymaking in the 1920s

*The horse-drawn rake was used to gather the hay as it lay on the ground after mowing. When enough had been collected, the prongs were raised, leaving ridges of hay to dry in lines across the field. Once dry, the hay was gathered (see below) and stored in ricks.*

*Hay mowing. The horses work in pairs. A long shaft extends forward between the horses from the mower. The harness is attached to a wooden cross piece called a whippletree (a wonderful word that deserves wider use!), which is, in turn, loosely, but securely, attached to the shaft.*

*This strange machine, a hay loader, was invented around 1910. Two sets of wooden battens with prongs move out of step with a combined motion along and at right-angles to a sloping surface. The combined motions caused the hay to be picked up and transferred to the top of the load on the wagon. The drive came from the forward motion provided by the horse.*

*Building a hayrick in the 1920s. Two horses are involved: one has pulled the load of hay so it can be unloaded on to the elevator. The horse stands tethered beyond on the left. The other horse is providing the power to operate the elevator. Its harness is attached to one end of a pole. The other end is fixed to a large toothed wheel, about 5 feet in diameter. As the horse walks round and round in a circle, the downward pointing teeth in the large wheel engage with and rotate a smaller cog-wheel and shaft. This shaft is at ground level, the other end engaging with the elevator, gradually raising the load of hay to the top of the hayrick. This mechanism was widely and successfully used on farms at the time. After the war a small Lister diesel engine was used to operate the elevator.*

*A horse-drawn hoe is being used in this picture. The crop has not been identified, possibly young cabbage or kale. In the background there is a railway embankment, with a few goods wagons. Some buildings dot the skyline. The scene may be on land later taken over by the Bristol Aeroplane Company.*

*A horse-drawn side-rake moving hay into ridges to speed up the drying process. The hay was moved by four or five angled pronged wheels, the hay passing from one wheel to the next.*

The 1930s had been a particularly challenging and difficult time for farmers. The damaging economic aftermath of the 1929 Wall Street crash was followed by years of very slow recovery. With the impending war and its declaration in 1939, a new economic outlook affected the country, with the need for less reliance on imported food. Land that had been left fallow was put to the plough. Every farmer was expected to grow significantly more food to feed the people of Britain. This was impossible to achieve while relying solely on real horse power. In 1941 a brand-new bottle-green Fordson tractor first arrived, bearing its Gloucestershire number plate, EDF 612. Although it quickly took over the heavier duties, usually with Bert Williams at the wheel, horses continued to play their part, drawing wagons, side-rakes and other farm machinery. But the use of horses was in decline: a second tractor was bought in 1954, and soon there was only one horse, Blossom, left.

Next in importance were the cattle. There was a regular herd of some sixty milking cows, pure-bred Friesians in the 1940s. They were milked twice each day, every day of the year, without exception. My father rose early every morning at six, often sneezing loudly as he went down stairs, ensuring that I, too, was awake. In winter the cows were waiting in their sheds in the various yards, while in summer they had to be brought in from one of the nearby grazing fields and led to their stalls. The

*1908: Cattle in the Home Field. Clay Bottom is behind the trees on the left.*

*Clockwise from the top left: Ben Weaver and bull. Two cows — a photographic record was kept of every cow on the farm in the 1920s. Feeding time in the old orchard at Clay Bottom — first there were three, then eight!*

cows were then milked, each one by hand, as it had always been done with head pressed into the cow's flank, the first pair of teats were worked until all the milk had been collected in the pail, gripped between the knees, all to be repeated with the other two teats. Milking was usually finished by 8:30 am. The fresh milk was carried in the special cylinder-shaped pails in which it had been collected from each cow. A record was kept of what each cow produced, and the milk was then passed through a cooler in the dairy at the back of the farmhouse. It was then stored in standard farm churns for daily collection by lorry. The process of cooling was important; markedly changing and improving the milk's flavour. All this before breakfast! At four in the afternoon the whole cycle was repeated.

Cows joined the milking herd after producing at least one calf, a process that seemed to turn on the 'milk tap', so to speak. For the females, they graduated from calves to yearlings to heifers, and then, with motherhood, to fully mature cows, in milk. The males calves followed a rockier path. Very few ever became full-grown bulls. Most would suffer the indignity of castration, growing up to become steers, their short lives terminated early to provide meat for consumption.

Each cow had its own unique name, for example, *Little Stoke Blackberry 34th*, and detailed records were kept of the bull, cows and the calves they produced. One bull was always kept on the farm for breeding. However sometimes cows produced their calves following artificial insemination. I got used to recognising the vet's car, so knew when this was happening.

Before the Second World War, the farm reared and maintained a large flock of sheep. The start of the housing development in Rossall Avenue and Kingsway on land between the lower part of Little Stoke Lane and the railway, made this increasingly difficult. Instances of dog worrying resulted in an ever-growing loss of sheep and lambs. It became uneconomic to continue, and the flock was sold.

A row of three pigsties stood alongside the dairy building. These provided dry indoor spaces for the animals with a low opening to small walled pens at the front. I remember their use for rearing pigs, but they were ill-suited for the more modern

*1913: Sheep were reared up to the mid-1930s. Harry Ponting is on the right by the horse and cart.*

*1937: Two pages from Harry Ponting's notebook — note 'ewe torn about by dogs'. (J. Thawley)*

methods of pig farming. With the decline in the number of horses, the barn stables were converted into a piggery, with special overhead electric lamps to provide warmth for newly born piglets. Pigs are the most intelligent of all farm animals – chickens and sheep perhaps the least. In some religions pigs are considered to be unclean and unfit to eat; however they are the only farmyard beasts to organise their living space so that only one part or corner is fouled. Where they lie and sleep is always relatively clean. Whereas cows will produce a single calf at a time, a sow's litter might comprise 9¾ piglets, the last one (the '¾'), the runt of the litter, was often smaller than the rest, and had to be watched and tended, if it was to survive. Sows, unless due precautions are taken, can sit on and squash the life out of one or more of their offspring. The new sties included a sturdy low rail, about nine inches above the floor, and a similar distance out from the sty walls behind which the young piglet could retreat when about to be sat upon. No photographs of the pigs at Little Stoke survive.

*Geese and chickens at Little Stoke Farm: winter and summer scenes.*

As for the rest, there were many hens, providing a plentiful supply of eggs. At one time the hens were truly free range, roaming the yards at will. They tended to ignore the nest boxes in their hen houses, and lay their eggs in private, secret places about the farm. Sometimes such a place was discovered with well over a dozen eggs in it! I also remember at least one very noisy cockerel. There were a dozen or so Khaki Campbell ducks: a breed, derived from the common Mallard, renowned for its capacity to lay eggs in large numbers; and a small flock, of perhaps up to nine, geese under the watchful eye of a mean-minded gander. He needed to be watchful because, a few days before each Christmas, one goose went missing. Every spring at least one gosling was hatched to grow and take its place.

There were cats living wild on the farm, with mice on their menus. Towards the end of our time at Little Stoke, I remember three of them, one with a missing leg, but no less agile than the others for all that. (I will spare you the distress of learning how that leg was lost). Finally, there were two domestic cats that shared the warmth and comfort of the house, together with the excitement and danger to be found on the farm!

*   *   *   *   *

# Little Stoke in Colour

*A watercolour of an old oak tree, painted by Mabel Davis in 1944, looking from Oaklands towards Savages Wood in the far distance. Braydon Avenue now runs across the scene in front of the tree. The tree and hedge are part of an ancient open field boundary created by the Saxons.*

*The towering elm trees in the snow-covered Homefield dwarf the farmhouse beyond.*

*The farmhouse in the snow, as the postman delivers the mail.*

*The farmhouse and garden in springtime.*

*The garden, by the front gate.*

*By the main farm gate.*

*The farm entrance early on an icy February morning in 1954.*

*Entrance to the Rickyard. The red cottages in the distance are still there, the only surviving buildings of the old Little Stoke hamlet.*

*The east side of Savages Wood looking towards the site of the future Bradley Stoke Community School, painted by Ernest P Bucknall around 1930.*

*A cabbage field at Little Stoke Farm, also painted by Ernest P Bucknall around 1930.*

# The Goose with the Golden Eyes

*A Lesser White-front, photographed at Slimbridge, April 2009, by Joe Blossom, reproduced with his kind permission.*

# Chapter 6

# Winter

Snow fell briefly at Little Stoke at some time during most winters, rarely making much impact, before melting quickly away. The snow could arrive late, as it did on April 1st 1921, covering the farm to a depth of two to three inches: but January and February were the usual months for snow.

At some other times the nights were star-filled and icy. In the mornings tiny pools in the footprints left by cattle had frozen over. Where the water beneath was able to drain away, the ice left behind, white, like frosted glass, would crunch appealingly as one walked in the yard. There were dangers: ridges left by cart wheels were hard and slippery. Meanwhile the ducks and geese trod gingerly on the cold ice that had suddenly covered their watery world.

*Above: Late winter snows at Little Stoke on April 1st 1921.*

Walking across the fields, one's eye was caught by the frost tinged grass, and by the hoar frost on the hedgerows. It was a magical world, particularly within the remote silent stillness of Savages Wood. It was, however, winter, and winters can be fickle: they can be dull and overcast, colourless, sometimes wet and foggy. In the late January of 1947 it was particularly fickle, challenging the very fabric of farming. On

*Winter 1947: Four scenes. The snow that settled was up to 9 inches deep, but when carried by the wind, the drifts were very deep. Bottom left shows the drift outside the farmhouse back door.*

January 22$^{nd}$ the temperature was around freezing and snow started to fall, blanketing the whole farm. The covering of snow lasted, uninterrupted, until March 12$^{th}$. The average depth of the snow that settled, rather than drifted, was around four inches over seven long weeks and, at its deepest, around nine inches. For almost two months the temperature rarely rose above freezing. It was the worst winter of the 20$^{th}$ century, both before 1947 and since: a winter like no other. It was, of course, an exciting time!

*1947: Above and left,: drifting snow in Cronnies. Below, Little Stoke Lane, blocked!*

*Winter 1954/55: Teazle stalks and winter snow.*

*Winter 1954/55: Cattle and haystack in the snow in Back Cowhouse.*

Little Stoke was affected by its severity, as were all the other farms. Cattle were kept on their beds of straw in the various cow sheds. The straw and their own body heat kept them warm. They had need of exercise and this was confined to the icy yards. The barn machinery worked overtime to produce enough fodder.

Sometimes when the snow came, it was carried on the wind. Parts of Little Stoke Lane became impassable, and there were drifts, many feet deep, near the hedgerows in some fields, none more so than by the hedge in Cronnies, adjoining the lane.

The wind would howl as it swirled past the farmhouse backdoor and up over the dairy. When laden with snow, the wind would again build up more deep drifts, blocking the path to the main yard.

Spring did arrive, late of course, but not before the crisp whiteness had turned to dirty slush. When spring's fresh shoots started to show, the worst winter in living memory was over.

There was a brief heavy fall of snow in the winter of 1954/5. No doubt people shook their heads and wondered if there was about to be a repeat of the harsh times in 1947. No, the snows soon melted away.

In the rest of this chapter the many photographs of the 1947 and 1955 winters tell their own stories.

*1947: Left: geese under watchful eye of William Cutler. Above and below: snow scenes in Savages Wood.*

*1947: Snowballs just outside Savages Wood, with school friend John Walters (right).*

*1947: The farmhouse, looking sombre, under a fresh fall of snow.*

*1955: Work to be done! A glimpse through the hedge into Moon Hayes from the Old Rough Ground, with tall elm trees in the distance.*

*1955: The track leading into Front Cowhouse from Moon Hayes, in the snow.*

*Left 1955: Stoke Lane looking from the farm towards Stoke Lodge.*

*Below: the same view in spring 2008*

*1955: The farmhouse under a blanket of fresh snow.*

*1947: Looking across Oaklands to the cottages at Little Stoke. Braydon Avenue now runs across this snow-covered scene, just beyond the gate.*

*1955: The second entrance to the farm between the kitchen garden and the farmhouse.*

*1955: Christopher and Peter Knapp, in the snow by the farm entrance.*

*1955: Sledging in Little Stoke Lane (now Clay Lane).*

*1955: The paperboy delivers.*

*Winter 1954/55: Ben Weaver's Cottage and Homefield elm trees*

# Chapter 7

# The Farm in Wartime

With the outbreak of war things changed on the farm. The nation needed to increase its home-grown supply of food, both in 1914 and 1939. There is no surviving documentation or photographs to show how these changes affected the farm during the First World War. How much those working there knew about the slaughter in the trenches in France, remains unknown. With radio or television yet to be invented, they would have had to rely on newspapers that reported, no doubt, selectively. My father, Howard, was called up for military service near the end of the war. Mercifully it ended before he was due to be dispatched from Catterick to France.

The impact of the Second World War was both similar and different. Similar in that there was the same need to produce more; different in that this time the war came to the farm, but not immediately. Before the war farming methods were essentially those of Victorian times. Gradually the internal combustion engine and electricity made their impact; however farmers of the BBC's Victorian Farm would have felt at home on many pre-war farms. The war changed this significantly.

The main London to South Wales railway was only two hundred yards from the farm. Beyond, near Gipsy Patch Lane was the expanding Bristol Aeroplane Company, which designed and built a number of key wartime aircraft, both fighters and bombers, for the Royal Air Force. This, quite understandably, provided two targets for the Luftwaffe in the same place!

*1942: 'Sowing for Victory'. Howard Davis is loading the seed drill. I look on from the tractor, which is driven by Bert Williams.*

*About 1943: The homefield where 20 bombs exploded on the night of August 22<sup>nd</sup> 1940. The elm trees were undamaged, as was Patchway Station, seen beyond the trees on the right.*

The first air-raid that affected the farm was in 1940, on the night of August 17th. In all, only seven bombs fell on the farmland, in a line coming in from the east, the last one landing just outside Bert Williams' cottage. This and five of the others all failed to explode. Phyllis Knapp, now 96, then living at Rose Dene cottage, recalls the discovery by the bomb disposal unit that the bomb near her house had no detonator: in its place a friendly message on scrap of paper from a worker in the factory in Czechoslovakia, where the bomb was assembled. The empty case of the

*August and September 1940: The above map, now fragile, shows where bombs fell on Little Stoke Farm. The intended targets were the Bristol Aeroplane Company and the South Wales railway. Each bomb is marked with a dark dot. Six dots, roughly in a line running east to west have circles around them. These six bombs all failed to explode, the last landing in the lane very close to the cottages where the Williams and Weaver families lived. The significance of the dots with ticks is not known.*

- 85 -

last bomb served as a stop by the back door, holding it firmly open when needed. Too heavy to lift, it stood some two feet tall, pointing skywards on its flat tail.

The bombers returned at night on August 22nd when 38 bombs fell on the farm. Two unoccupied houses in Little Stoke were demolished. There were further raids on the night of September 4th and during the daytime, on the 25th. Over 50 bombs landed on Little Stoke Farm on these four raids alone. In total, some 70 bombs landed on the farmland inflicting minimal damage and, mercifully, no loss of life. Howard Davis marked where each bomb landed on an old map, including a cluster in Savages Wood! A water-filled crater still remains there, behind the Bradley Stoke Leisure Centre. (See Appendix 7 for more details about the raids).

Visits by the Luftwaffe had been anticipated. Some tall gun towers were erected to protect the airfield — one, at the end of the large field in front of the farm. A Royal Air Force barrage balloon site was set up close to the farmhouse in May 1940,

*Summer 1942: Part of the cider press has just been moved from Clay Bottom, using wooden posts acting as rollers, to the farmhouse garden gate by the RAF personnel stationed at the Little Stoke barrage balloon site.*

with its tethered large silver-grey balloon. This was one of 24 set up for the protection of the Filton area, with its aircraft industry. Lighter than air, each balloon could be made to float, a leviathan of the sky, at the end of its long cable. Its purpose was to force the bombers to fly higher, making them easier targets for the anti-aircraft gunners.

Bomb craters were an unsightly problem. On the morning of August 23rd there were 20 of them, made by high explosive bombs, in the 30 acre field facing the house; most were closer to the railway than to Little Stoke Lane. Both the barrage balloon site and the gun tower were undamaged and, even more remarkably, all 60 cows were led to their stalls for milking! It was the daytime raid on September 25th that caused much devastation: tragically there were 131 fatalities at the Bristol Aeroplane Company, out of a total of 135 during the war. Fortunately only three bombs struck the farm fields in that raid.

The craters did not stay long. Guarded groups of prisoners from a nearby prisoner of war camp duly filled them in with pick axe and shovel. It became apparent that although many prisoners were supporters of Hitler's dream, others had no heart or liking for the war that they had been forced to join. Sometimes the guards would borrow an old saucepan and other vessels to help with food preparation. Once my mother plucked up courage and asked a guard whether there was anyone interesting in the group of prisoners; perhaps a risky question. The guard replied that there was a doctor from Vienna who had been forced to join the German Army — "I'll send him back with the pots", he is alleged to have added. The doctor duly returned the utensils later, and was grateful to have the

*1943: The old cider press installed as a water feature in the front garden. The cider press dates from the early 1700s.*

opportunity to meet my parents. When the war was over, Dr. Hans Kiesling wrote to them at the farm, recalling the incident and thanking them for their kindness. A long friendship followed and one of the earliest visitors to stay, when my parents moved to Clapton in Gordano, was the doctor's teenage daughter.

Although the bombing of the farm had ended by spring 1941, the barrage balloon site continued to be manned for a while; the balloon tethered at ground level. The men were organised to occupy their time constructively. There was a fitness instructor, as well as a pommel horse and exercise rings hanging from a nearby tree. The rough pasture surrounding the Nissen and wooden huts was tamed to grow an abundance of vegetables. There was even a lawn and flower garden.

One activity involving the balloon site personnel is still vivid in my mind. Down at Clay Bottom, in the small paddock opposite, barely visible amongst the tall grass and nettles, was an old stone cider press. It came in three parts. Two semicircular blocks which, when fitted together and sealed, formed a circular trough about seven feet in diameter at its outer edge. The third part was a large stone wheel, which could stand in the trough. A long wooden pole would have passed through its central hole. At one end, the pole was pivoted on a short upright post in the middle of the trough, at the other, was a horse. As the horse trudged its circular path the stone wheel turned, crushing the juice out of the cider apples in its path. My mother had eyed this press as an excellent garden ornament, and so it turned out to be.

Its three parts were well dug in, camouflaged by long grass and nettles. With the secure protection of a strong stone wall, it lay hidden like a three man advance reconnaissance party ahead of an invasion. It had an open view of the railway, the roofs of the aircraft works some distance beyond, as well as the barrage balloon through the trees. A military solution was needed, to be provided by the men from the balloon site. Plans of attack were drawn up, and defensive weaknesses identified.

On the day, armed only with shovels and strong wooden and iron stakes, the RAF moved in from the south and east of the paddock. The three stone pieces, once secure in their dugout, were quickly over-run, surrendering their firm grip in the ground. Hauled out into the lane, the captive pieces were, in turn, bound with strong ropes and lifted onto ten or so round fence posts laid parallel across the lane. Like this, the lorry could easily pull the each stone forward, the poles rolling beneath it. As a pole emerged at the back it had to be picked up and placed just in front of the stone to repeat its role. In this way all three captive stones reached the front gate. Here a new strategy was needed: the stone pieces, weighing tons, were pulled, sliding along smooth wooden boards, with co-ordinated military exertion through the gate into their final positions. The operation was over. I, aged only four, had watched everything from a safe distance. Fortunately my mother filmed it all with an old eight millimetre cine camera. The circular stone wheel became a low garden table, while the trough made a fine water feature, later surrounded by many plants.

In 1942 there was another very different addition to the farm, this time human. My parents had agreed to help a refugee family who had fled from Austria following the Nazi take-over. Like so many refugees who came to Britain, fleeing from the impending war, they were sent to the Isle of Man for assessment. Posing no threat, they returned to the mainland and arrived at Temple Meads Station. My father met them, finding them easily; four lost souls on a windy station in a foreign country, facing an uncertain future. Mrs Maendl and her three children, Godfrey, Beatrix and Andrew, spent what was for me, as an only child, a wonderful year on the farm. I think it was for them too. Later Andrew, the youngest, trained to be a doctor; I still know and see him to this day.

*Autumn 1942: Riding the Fordson Standard tractor— left to right; Beatrix Maendl, me, Bert Williams, his son David, and Andrew Maendl.*

The later war years passed without threatening incidents; just farming to produce more food. Family holidays were, of course, out of the question - the best one could hope for was an odd day out at Weston-super-Mare, with a nervous ride on a donkey. One such occasion was in August 1944, with a school friend, Alan Holzer. His father was serving in the Royal Artillery, so Alan spent the whole summer break on the farm. He still has vivid memories of his time there...

*A wartime day out at Weston-super-Mare in 1944 with long standing friend, Alan (right), from school.*

'...In front of the farmhouse, the other side of a lane, was a large green field, with a group of very tall elm trees in the middle. Then, down to the right, a railway cutting where the trains came through on their way to Bristol, straining up the bank. The English engines, GWR and LMS, puffed in the English way, with great gouts of smoke and steam coming out of their chimneys, but the American ones, ugly, black-painted monsters with strange wheel configurations like 0-8-0 or 4-12-4, made an eerie, shrieking sound because they burnt oil instead if coal. There were some huts in the field and, for a time, French workers were housed in them. These workers gave Martin and me our first (and if Mrs Davis had had her way, our last) taste of chewing gum, little rectangular pieces covered in a white sugar crust. I don't know about chewing gum losing its flavour on the bedpost overnight, but we kept those pieces going for a fortnight!

I remember the house well — the grey stone and the waving beds of irises along the wall. Indoors were the usual rooms and one, in a way, magic room. I remember it as a late discovery, going with Martin along corridors and down and up little stairways and there was this room which appeared to have no connection with the others. In it were toys — a German cable railway, a clockwork Hornby train set, and a wind-up gramophone. We found a record of the William Tell overture and set the gramophone to work. But the wretched thing would wind down just at the pitch of the storm so that instead of great thunder blasts of music we got, despite frantic attempts at the winding handle, just a series of deathly groans. Then there was the bird bath in the garden, made from a cider-press. I am sure that the birds were happy enough with it, but we had other ideas. The precious Hornby train was put together, complete with engine, tender, carriages, trucks, guards van, station, signals, luggage trolleys and porters — under water. The engine, duly wound up, bravely hauled the train around once, twice, a bit more and gave up.

A farm in 1944 was wonderland, not the sterile, Health and Safety regulated, empty, lifeless agribusiness complex it is now. I am sure we were under the watchful eye of some Little Stoke Farm god since we never came to any harm, for all the daft things we did. One morning we might wage a battle to the death against the stinging nettles round the pond, hacking and bashing with sticks, the ducks utterly bewildered by the shower of nettle leaves which fell around them. We watched chickens have their necks broken before being plucked. We ate cow cake. We worked the mangel-cutter (under supervision). We made tunnels through the hay in the dutch barn. We watched as a gander went for Pa Davis, pecking at his leg. This was no Ladybird Book farm, I can tell you.

Farms are, of course muddy and, in due course Mrs Davis decided that "Alan must have a pair of Wellington boots". I did not know what Wellington boots were, but Wellingtons I must have. So off we go to Thombury in Mrs Davis' fawn Austin 10. It being war time Wellingtons were, if not rationed by coupons, very much in short supply. But Wellingtons Alan needed and Wellingtons Alan would get. The shop girl who attended to us hadn't a chance. A mixture of skilled rhetoric and awesome special pleading (not for nothing did Mrs Davis later become a magistrate) did the job and I got my wellies.

Martin has written of the outing to Weston-super-Mare, but he didn't mention the sinking paddle boat. I guess Mrs Davis thought we were old enough to go out on the boating lake by ourselves. It was a grey, wet day and no one else had hired a boat. Once we had worked out how not to go round and round in circles we bravely headed out to the centre of the lake. Then the boat began to leak, going down slowly at one end. We paddled frantically, managing all of what must have been half a knot an hour, and got within a few yards of the side of the lake when the boat sank, resting in about six inches of muddy water.

The farm had, when I was first there, three German prisoners of war, two young men and an older fellow called Hans. Hans was bad-tempered and lazy, always grumbling and going on about all the work he had to do. Somehow Hans had picked up a pair of boots he wanted to take back to Germany for his son. They were old-fashioned hob-nailed boots, with rows of studs across the soles and were smeared with dubbin to keep the wet out. One day Hans got me on my own and indicated that I should wear-in the boots so that they would be comfortable for his son. This I was to do by walking in them round the farm all day. The boots weren't very comfortable but I managed to walk in them until about tea-time when Mrs Davis found me and spotted the boots. I got a reprimand, but done in a very kindly way, more explaining that I was putting Mrs Davis in a difficult position by my action, however well intended. And Hans was allowed to keep the boots.

I would like to express, on behalf of myself, my father, the Maendl family, and many others who benefited in such a wonderful way, a great sense of gratitude for the kindness and hospitality shown by Mr and Mrs Davis, especially during the war years, but also for many years beyond. They were special times.'

*Above, October 1936: View looking north in Broadmead, towards Gipsy Patch Lane on an overcast day. Patchway Station footbridge is just visible, right of centre.*

*Below, March 1954: The same view from about five hundred feet. The dark roofs of the Shadow factory, built just before WW2, run from the centre to the left. Beyond Gipsy Patch Lane, lies the Bristol Aeroplane Company's Engine Division, built after the war: to its right, Patchway Station.*

*The above two photographs are reproduced with kind permission of the Rolls-Royce Heritage Trust.*

Soon after the war had ended, the Anderson shelter and all its attendant sandbags were taken out of the drawing room. Building re-started near Rossall Avenue and Little Stoke Lane, first with the erection of prefabs and gradually more permanent housing, and a few shops opened near Gipsy Patch Lane. Little Stoke Infants and Junior Schools were added in the early 1950s.

*About 1953: Harvesting in Sternbridges, the new Little Stoke Junior/Infants school beyond.*

What happened to those parts of the farm west of the railway, purchased during the 1930s by the Bristol Aeroplane Company in two lots, north and south of Gipsy Patch Lane? In 1935 as a result of government planning for the threatening clouds of war, a country-wide programme of the construction of 'shadow factories' was initiated. These would provide for a rapid increase in war effort production if or

*By the early 1950s only one solitary Nissen Hut (right) stood to remind us of the Balloon site.*

when war was declared. The large dark roofed sheds in the lower photograph on page 92, built in the late 1930s were part of this programme. These sheds, five in all, were subject to much bombing in the early years of the war (see Appendix 7).

And lastly, what of the Balloon site and the servicemen stationed there; men who, in a sense, had become part of the life of the farm itself? They were rotated on to other tours of duty, not all surviving the war. The buildings were like forgotten sentinels standing guard over the new post-war order of austerity and ration cards. The wooden ones were the first to go, then those with brick walls. By the early 1950s one lone Nissen hut stood as a sole reminder of but a brief period in Little Stoke's long history.

\*   \*   \*   \*   \*

*Early 1940s: Elm trees on Little Stoke Farm*

# Chapter 8

# Harvest Time

Harvest time was the culmination of the farmer's year; a time when all the strands of diverse labours came together. The bringing in of the harvest was, and often still is, celebrated in churches with traditional Harvest Festival services.

Of course there was not just one harvest time, but a series, which depended on what was grown. At Little Stoke, during the time Howard Davis farmed the land, this had three elements: the hay harvest; the cereal harvest, oats, barley and wheat; and lastly the root crop harvest, mangels, swedes, turnips and potatoes. These would happen in that order: haymaking in June and July, cereals in August and September, followed by the root crops. Of these harvests, the most exciting, by far, was the cereal harvest, particularly for a growing boy!

Hay-making too brought joy, so long as hay-fever was not a problem. It had not been for me, nor for others on the farm, as far as I know. The to- and fro- cutting action of the horse- or tractor-drawn mower would soon lay a once up-right swaying grass crop into neat flat rows. The hay had to dry out before it could be safely stored in thatched ricks. If the stems and long narrow leaves were not sufficiently dry within the hayrick, decomposition would start to generate heat: if the conditions were right, enough to cause smouldering followed eventually by fire.

Side rakes would arrange the hay in loose ridges in the field, about a foot to eighteen inches high. Sometimes the fast rotating rakes of a tedder would scatter the hay to help it to dry much faster. Once the hay was dry, the rick building would start. The cream coloured elevator would be woken from its slumber in a corner of one of the yards, nettles starting to grow around its rusting wheels. It had last seen action eight months earlier and creaked a bit. Its moving parts oiled, it would be towed to its appointed place. Unfolded, its long smooth sloping ramp would be set at a low angle for the rick building to begin. As the rick grew, the angle would be made a bit steeper. Two chains ran up the sides of the ramp. Strung between them, narrow wooden battens, with fearsome upward pointing rusty iron spikes, would carry the hay to the top, where it was received, usually by two men, who moved the hay to its final position in the growing rick before the next load arrived. Once started, the work was dusty and continuous except for meal breaks and, of course, for the cows, which had to be milked.

*Hay rick building in the early 1950s. Brian Knapp, right.*

The hay, in its loose ridges strung out across the meadow, was collected in the low horizontal long iron-tipped prongs (or tines) of a sweep attached to an open topped old car, and delivered to the base of the elevator. One model used was an old Alvis: it would be worth a fortune now! Later a tractor was used instead.

*1930s: Reaping by binder, drawn by a three-horse team.*

*1955: Jim Wyatt and Howard Davis discuss a binder problem.*

*1955: The binder at work near Sherbourne's Brake. Stoke Brook is hidden from view on the right.*

The top of each rick was finished with a pyramid shape, to be thatched, usually by Benjamin Weaver. The hay was for the cows, forming, with other harvested crops, part of their nourishing winter feed. The cows too, were well looked after.

The cereal harvest usually followed hard on the end of haymaking. The increased output of the Second World War continued into peacetime. Oddly there are very

*1955: Reaping close to Stoke Brook. Just above the tractor bonnet, on the horizon, is the outline of St. Michael's Church in Stoke Gifford. Jim Wyatt on the binder, John Cook, driving.*

*1955: Building stooks in Footbridges near Stoke Brook.. The footbridge rail is just visible. Left to right: Howard Davis, Bill Cutler, Ben Weaver and John Cook.*

*1955: Building a rick of unthreshed wheat in Front Cowhouse. John Cook and Jim Wyatt on the rick; Howard Davis is on the ladder.*

few surviving photographs of harvesting earlier, although the farm inventories, drawn up when the farm changed hands, clearly show that cereal crops were grown. Perhaps it played a smaller role, the grain only being used in cattle feed and the straw for their bedding. Edward Davis was primarily a dairy farmer, but he did grow the supporting crops. It is clear that, in Sidney Witchell's time and that of Benjamin Willcox before him, some land was arable. John Player in around 1750 recorded that, on taking over Phillips's Matford, the first crop grown was wheat. There had, therefore, been an arable tradition for at least 200 years.

When the barley, oats or wheat were judged ripe, the Massey Harris binder was towed crab-like to the field. Crab-like, because it was otherwise too wide for the farm gates. Sideways on, with extra wheels, was fine. The first sight I had of this complex machine was when it was pulled by a team of four or five horses. There was a long wooden shaft, with shorter strong wooden cross-pieces called whippletrees, their centres pivoted on the main shaft. The harness of each horse was attached carefully to the whippletree. The horses then pulled, and had to do so equally. The person in charge required real skill. A great sight; less so when the more efficient Fordson Standard tractor took over.

Thin slowly rotating paddles on the binder bent the stalks back as they were cut by the blades moving side to side below. The parallel fallen stalks were carried by moving canvas belts, first to one side, to make room for more, and then up to a holding space. When sufficient had gathered, long fast moving spikes carrying string, called binder twine, quickly tied the corn into sheaves. A set of rotating prongs then cast each sheaf on to the ground.

A team of people, farm hands, family and friends — harvesting was then labour intensive — picked up the sheaves, arranging them in stooks, either six or eight quietly leaning against each

*Early 1940s: A line of ricks awaiting the arrival of the threshing machine.*

other, like revellers from a party, lightly tipsy, but not too drunk to fall over. In this state the stooks would dry out, like the party goers, prior to another round of rick building.

The next stage would be threshing; in a sense the climax of the harvest season, but not its end. The huge boxlike machines were hired from specialist contractors. Where these machines came from, I had no idea back in the 1940s. Sometimes

*Autumn 1942: Threshing scenes at Little Stoke, in one of the two fields close to Savages Wood.*

*A relic of Victorian times, this old horse drawn wagon, here photographed in the summer of 1943, was in use until the mid-1950s.*

*Around 1955: Peter Knapp learning the craft of raking near Savages Wood.*

*1955: Christopher Knapp, Stan and Dorothy Cook watch the burning of surplus straw.*

*Autumn 1944: Harvesting the potato crop in Middledown. Moon Hayes field in the distance.*

they would arrive pulled by tractors, more powerful than our Fordson Standard, or by one of those old traction engines, now confined to steam rallies. With large metal wheels crunching along the lane, driven by a loud chugging steam engine, they travelled noisily: they were heard well before they were seen arriving at the farm gate.

Soon set up for action, with a long canvas belt, that swayed menacingly, transferring power from the tractor or traction engine to the threshing machine, its work would start by separating the ears of corn from the stalks, and in turn the grain from the ears and husks. Loose straw emerged high up on one end, falling on to the end of the elevator to be transformed into a new rick. Down low at the other end, the clean seeds of oats, barley or wheat poured out of small chutes into welcoming sacks. Other unwanted seeds and husks emerged from another chute onto the ground as waste. All this was achieved by hidden mechanical beaters and vibrating sieves, operated by a complexity of wheels and levers, visible to the onlooker.

The straw left over after threshing was often used as bedding for the livestock during the long winter months. In the times of higher production the excess straw was usually burnt. Some of the

*Early 1950s: A panoramic view of Savages Wood, from Lower Savages. The new Bradley Stoke Community School is now just out of sight on the right. The new Town Centre obscures the view, including the cows and haystack, in the left hand half of the picture.*

sacks of barley, oats and corn were sold to corn merchants; they always sought the best quality, but only after sufficient had been stored in the barn, with its mill, to be ground into flour to be added to the winter cattle food mixture.

The final harvest was the gathering in of the root crops. This was done the old-fashioned way, by hand: slow arduous and back-breaking. Turnips, mangels and swedes were loaded into carts and stored in an enormous sloping heap at the back of the barn.

*Lifting the root-crop. Harry Ponting, with horse and cart on land now part of Bradley Stoke, probably in the 1920s. (J. Thawley)*

At the end of the season the corn stubble was ploughed back in. Harrows (zigzag and disc) and rollers (flat or ring) were used to break up the soil, ready for the sowing of winter and spring crops or clover, if the soil needed to be enriched, bringing the harvest season to a timely end.

\* \* \* \* \*

# The Final Cut

*This dramatic photograph was taken around 1930, and shows the binder at Little Stoke pulled by a team of three shire horses. The binder is about to reap the final small patch of a mixture of wheat and barley. A scene such as this would have occurred on farms across the country from the 1880s, when this form of mechanised reaping was first introduced. (Photo from the Ponting family, lent by Dorothy Burden)*

# Chapter 9

# Wildlife and its Champion

Savages Wood and the farm hedgerows were nurtured by Howard Davis as havens for wildlife. The hedgerows clearly had a more hum-drum importance: to keep livestock in. The law added an incentive: escaping cattle can cause damage and accidents, and fines were imposed. This happened at least once to my father, and probably more often. An inconsiderate walker, leaving a gate open or unlatched, was no excuse!

In 1896 Savages was young for a wood, perhaps not more than 50 years old. In 1842 it had not even been planted; in its place, a field called Savers. This may have been two or three smaller fields earlier. If you look carefully when walking in the wood there are oaks that must pre-date it. They tend to be in lines, as if part of an old hedge, their branches spreading widely. This spread would not have happened had they grown from seedlings amongst other woodland trees. Of the three woods in Bradley Stoke, it is the youngest.

Farming was Howard's livelihood, but natural history, particularly the study of birds, was his passion. Not one of his school reports has survived, but he always said that he had three absorbing interests at school: history, natural history and cricket. It was his destiny, and perhaps his family duty, to take up the reins of farming. The die was cast, subjects that did not interest him passed him by. When he began working seriously on the farm he had to do what Edward, his father, demanded of him. When in the fields, however, he found the time to learn how to see nature, and to understand its sounds and movements. It took time and effort to discover these things. He was self-taught, reading books on birds over and over again, until he was able to recognise every bird that he saw. He also learned how to identify them from their birdsong, a more difficult task.

*Late 1940s. Above and below left, scenes in Savages Wood in the early spring. Below right, a winter scene, now obscured by the Bradley Stoke Library and Leisure Centre.*

When Howard took over, he was in total charge of the farm, although his father still owned it. He kept records of the wildlife he saw between 1931 and 1947, without in any way neglecting the farm.

## List of Mammals
noted (as up to 8.8.47)

Noctule Bat
Pipistrelle (bat)
Whiskered Bat
Long-eared Bat
Hedgehog
Mole
Common Shrew
Pigmy Shrew
Water Shrew
Brown Hare
Rabbit
Red Squirrel
Grey Squirrel
Field Mouse
House Mouse
Brown Rat
Water Vole
Field Vole
Bank Vole
Weasel
Stoat
Fox
Badger

## List of Butterflies
noted (as up to 26.7.47)

Speckled Wood
Wall
Marbled White
Hedge Brown
Meadow Brown
Small Heath
Silver-washed fritillary
Red Admiral
Painted Lady
Small Tortoiseshell
Peacock
Comma
White Admiral
Brown Argus
Common Blue
Holly Blue
Small Copper
Green Hairstreak
Purple Hairstreak
White-letter Hairstreak
Large White
Small White
Green-veined White
Orange Tip
Clouded Yellow
Brimstone
Grizzled Skipper
Large Skipper

*Lists of mammals and butterflies seen at Little Stoke by Howard Davis. Note the red squirrel.*

| LITTLE STOKE FM. Arrival dates - spring migrants 1931 - 1947 | 1931. | 1932. | 1933. | 1934. | 1935. | 1936. | 1937. | 1938. |
|---|---|---|---|---|---|---|---|---|
| Tree-Pipit | Apr.25. | Apr.24. | Apr.15. | Apr.19 | Apr.19. | Apr.24. | Apr.24 | Apr.17. |
| Yellow Wagtail | Apr.11. | Apr.24. | Apr.15. | Apr.15. | Apr.20 | Apr.17 | Apr.10. | Apr.8. |
| White Wagtail | - | - | Apr.15 | Apr.17. | - | - | - | - |
| Red-backed Shrike | - | - | - | May.28 | May.15 | May.21 | - | - |
| Spotted Flycatcher | May.6. | May.14. | May.3. | May.13 | May.13 | May.5. | May.10 | May.17 |
| Pied Flycatcher | - | - | - | - | - | - | - | Apr.30 |
| Chiffchaff | Mar.19. | Mar.25. | Mar.25. | Apr.7. | Mar.23. | Mar.27. | Mar.24. | Mar.18. |
| Willow-Warbler | Apr.12. | Apr.14. | Apr.11. | Apr.12. | Apr.12 | Apr.1. | Apr.7. | Apr.10 |
| Wood-Warbler | - | - | - | - | - | - | - | - |
| Grasshopper-Warbler | - | - | - | - | - | - | - | - |
| Marsh-Warbler | - | - | - | - | June.15. | - | - | - |
| Sedge-Warbler | - | May.8. | May.3. | Apr.29 | - | - | - | - |
| Garden-Warbler | May.6. | May.23. | May.9. | May.11 | May.6. | May.3. | May.5. | May.20. |
| Blackcap | May.1. | Apr.23. | Apr.22. | Apr.21. | Apr.12. | Apr.14. | Apr.24. | Apr.9. |
| Whitethroat | Apr.25. | Apr.25. | Apr.18. | Apr.19 | Apr.20. | Apr.22. | Apr.20. | Apr.22 |
| Lesser Whitethroat | - | - | May.12 | Apr.23 | Apr.24 | Apr.29 | Apr.21. | May.5 |
| Wheatear | Mar.26 | Apr.8. | Mar.25. | Apr.6. | Apr.16. | Mar.30. | Mar.29. | Apr.9. |
| Whinchat | May.1. | Apr.25. | Apr.15. | Apr.18. | Apr.20. | Apr.30. | Apr.28. | Apr.30. |
| Redstart | Apr.18 | Apr.23. | Apr.19. | Apr.20. | May.1. | - | Apr.10. | Apr.18. |
| Nightingale | - | - | - | - | - | Apr.28. | Apr.14. | Apr.25. |
| Swallow | Apr.12. | Apr.6. | Apr.7. | Apr.13. | Apr.9. | Apr.11. | Apr.9. | Apr.4. |
| House-Martin | Apr.25. | Apr.21. | Apr.15. | May.9. | Apr.22 | Apr.29. | Apr.25. | Apr.27. |
| Sand-Martin | May.2. | May.2. | Apr.29. | - | May.29. | - | - | May.9. |
| Swift | May.1. | Apr.22. | May.1. | Apr.21. | May.4. | May.3. | Apr.30. | May.15. |
| Cuckoo | Apr.25. | Apr.24. | Apr.22. | Apr.22 | Apr.22. | Apr.28. | Apr.28. | Apr.23. |
| Turtle-Dove | - | - | May.3. | May.23. | May.12. | May.3. | May.12 | May.15 |
| Common Sandpiper | - | - | - | - | - | - | - | - |
| Whimbrel | - | - | Apr.30. | May.3. | - | - | - | - |
| Lesser Blk-backed Gull. | Apr.26. | - | - | Apr.24 | - | Feb.18* | Mar.1. | - |

\* probably a wintering bird.

*Arrival dates of migrant birds, 1931 to 1938.  As recorded by Howard Davis.*

| LITTLE STOKE FM. Arrival dates – spring migrants 1931–1947 | 1939. | 1940. | 1941. | 1942. | 1943. | 1944. | 1945. | 1946. | 1947 |
|---|---|---|---|---|---|---|---|---|---|
| Tree-Pipit | Apr.29 | May 7. | — | — | May 13 | Apr.16 | May 5 | May18 | Apr.11 |
| Yellow Wagtail | Apr.11 | Apr.13 | Apr.20 | Apr.14 | Apr.18 | Apr.14 | Apr.18 | Apr.15 | Apr.26 |
| White Wagtail | — | Apr.21 | Apr.25 | — | — | — | — | — | — |
| Red-backed Shrike | — | — | — | — | June 6 | May 21 | — | — | — |
| Spotted Flycatcher | June 4 | May 15 | May 21 | May.1 | May 12 | May 8 | May 10 | May 12 | May 7 |
| Pied Flycatcher | — | — | — | — | — | Apr. 8 | — | — | |
| Chiffchaff | Mar.30 | Mar.23 | Mar.15 | Mar.21 | Mar 24 | Mar.27 | Mar.18 | Mar.23 | |
| Willow-Warbler | Apr 7 | Apr.13 | Apr 12 | Apr.11 | Mar.26 | Apr. 7 | Apr. 6 | Apr.7 | Apr.1 |
| Wood-Warbler | — | — | — | — | — | — | — | Apr.27 | — |
| Grasshopper-Warbler | | | | May 1. | — | — | — | — | — |
| Marsh-Warbler | — | — | — | — | — | — | — | — | |
| Sedge-Warbler | May20 | — | May 17 | Apr.25 | — | — | May 7 | Apr.29 | — |
| Garden-Warbler | May 8 | Apr.30 | May 4 | May 15 | Apr 28 | Apr.26 | Apr.21 | May 10 | Apr.28 |
| Blackcap | Apr.26 | Apr. 2 | Apr.30 | Apr.20 | Apr 3 | Apr.9 | Apr.16 | Apr.19 | Apr.26 |
| Whitethroat | Apr 15 | Apr.19 | Apr 21 | Apr.27 | Apr.18 | Apr.12 | Apr.13 | Apr.16 | Apr 13 |
| Lesser Whitethroat | Apr.21 | Apr.24 | Apr.26 | Apr.25 | Apr 25 | Apr.26 | Apr.15 | Apr.19 | Apr 18 |
| Wheatear | Mar 31 | Apr.2 | Apr.19 | Mar.28 | Mar.21 | Mar.27 | Apr 11 | Apr.29 | |
| Whinchat | Apr 25 | Apr.22 | Apr.29 | May10 | May 6 | Apr.22 | Apr.27 | Apr.29 | Apr.26 |
| Redstart | Apr 11 | Apr.9 | Apr.15 | Apr.19 | — | Apr.7 | Apr.11 | — | May 2 |
| Nightingale | Apr.29 | — | May 7 | Apr.25 | Apr.13 | Apr.14 | Apr.18 | Apr.27 | Apr.30 |
| Swallow | Apr.9 | Apr.20 | Apr.16 | Apr.18 | Apr.5 | Apr. 8 | Apr.5 | Apr.5 | Apr.19 |
| House-Martin | Apr.13 | Apr.24 | May 1 | May 2 | Apr.30 | Apr.12 | May 10 | June 1 | — |
| Sand-Martin | — | — | — | — | — | — | Apr.27 | Apr.27 | |
| Swift | May 12 | May 11 | May 7 | May 7 | May 1 | May 7 | May 6 | May 3 | May. 3 |
| Cuckoo | May 7 | Apr.29 | Apr.21 | Apr.21 | Apr.21 | Apr.16 | Apr.17 | Apr.14 | Apr.15 |
| Turtle-Dove | May 5 | May 4 | May 7 | May 23 | June 2 | May 12 | Apr.30 | May13 | May 29 |
| Common Sandpiper | Apr 22 | — | — | — | — | — | — | — | — |
| Whimbrel | — | — | May 1 | — | — | — | — | — | — |
| Lesser Black-backed Gull | Apr 29 | — | Mar 22 | May 15 | Mar.5 | Apr. 2 | Apr.4 | — | May 3 |

*Arrival dates of migrant birds, 1939 to 1947. As recorded by Howard Davis.*

When Edward Davis first rented the farm in 1896, the Beaufort Estate owned the hunting rights on the land. Later the Berkeley Hunt held traditional meets at various farms in the area, meeting at Little Stoke in December 1929. Before the hunt arrived an instruction was issued to block entrances to the foxes' earths . I do not know whether the day was a success for the hunt or the fox.

*Above: The meet of the Berkeley Hunt at Little Stoke Farm on December 16th 1929.*

*Left:
The Berkeley
Hunt spreads
out on the
farm at Little
Stoke.*

Whereas Edward probably viewed the hunt as a useful way of controlling foxes, reducing their detrimental impact on poultry and lambs, his son Howard, was not at ease with hunting. To him, if a fox caused problems it should be shot: there was no place for sentimentality in his approach to wildlife. He did, however, champion nature. He was 'green' before the term had entered the vocabulary; but he was practical. He owned a shot-gun, its use was confined to the odd fox and to scare wood pigeons in freshly seeded fields.

When he took over the farm in 1931, my father wanted to end hunting on its fields, and made his displeasure of it known. He took some stick from the local press: 'a young upstart farmer…'. He won. The hunt chased its foxes elsewhere.

Howard made his friendships with others who had like-minded interests in natural history, some of them were good photographers. Men like Harry Savory, R.P. Gait and Peter Gale, set up their hidden cameras on the farm, and photographed many of the birds.

*1948: Hen Sparrowhawk and its young at Sherbourne's Brake. Photograph by Peter Gale.*

My mother urged her husband to join the Bristol Naturalists' Society. He did, and after serving time on various committees, was made its president in 1951: a post normally held only once. His enthusiasm and industry called for an exception, and he was honoured with the presidency again in 1964, the Society's Centenary year.

He joined most of the important national ornithological organisations, such as the Royal Society for the Protection of Birds and the British Trust for Ornithology, working on many of their committees. He was on first name terms with leading ornithologists in the era following the end of the Second World War. Howard Davis was, however, a modest man: he never blew his own trumpet. I have heard other ornithologists say that he deserved greater recognition.

*1947: A Spotted Flycatcher at Little Stoke, photographed by R. P. Gait.*

*A Little Owl and young in the roof of the sheds in Front Cowhouse field, photographed by Peter Gale, probably in the late 1940s.*

Perhaps there was one achievement that meant more to him than all the others: his involvement with the creation of the Severn Wildfowl Trust, now the Wildlife and Wetlands Trust (WWT) at Slimbridge in Gloucestershire.

Between the world wars Slimbridge was a small quiet village, half a mile or so west of the main road between Bristol and Gloucester. About one mile beyond the village, the lane crossed the Sharpness to Gloucester canal, continuing as a track for a quarter of a mile, ending by a couple of cottages, some farm buildings

*1936: The grass track to the Dumbles at Slimbridge. The photograph was taken from where the In Focus shop now stands.*

and an old duck decoy. A rough grassy track led on from there to an earth embankment that protected the farmland from spring-tide flooding. Beyond this embankment stretched the Dumbles, as it was known, a large flat grass covered area that extended to the banks of the Severn Estuary. This was a remote area of little human activity. It did, however, and still does, provide a winter home for many varieties of migratory geese and ducks. In the summer months it was, and of course still is, the home of many wading birds. When not busy on the farm, Howard Davis had spent many hours lying on the earthen bank watching the geese through his old telescope. He knew the best places to view the geese, and so it was that he wrote to Peter Scott, (son of Robert Falcon Scott of Antarctic fame), who had run a wildfowl reserve in Norfolk before the war.

Peter Scott, who later received a knighthood for his work for nature conservation, wrote in his autobiography at the start of the chapter called Slimbridge Discovered:

'In the autumn of 1945 I received two letters from ornithologist friends which, taken in conjunction, were to have a very profound effect on my life. Both these letters were from farmers and both concerned wild geese. The first was from Howard Davis, an experienced observer of birds living near Bristol, who sent me a copy of a paper he had written on the great flock of White-fronted Geese which has wintered on the Severn Estuary from immemorial times. If I could spare the time to come down, he wrote, he would like to show them to me. I remembered my brief visit there before the war, at a time when the main flock had just left on the spring migration. I had seen, as I recalled, a bunch of twenty or thirty and that was all, and I had examined with interest the old duck decoy in the little wood. It would be nice to go there again, but I wondered when, if ever, there would be time.'

*1936: Howard Davis (right) watching geese over the earth embankment.*

They did meet, along with two of Peter's friends, John Winter and Clive Wilson, by the swing bridge over the Sharpness-Gloucester canal. They walked on along the track, past the cottages, soon reaching the Dumbles. A disused military pill-box, designed and built early in WW2 as a defensive post for a machine gunner, stood on the bank that protected the farmland through which they had just walked. They used its cramped space to view the large flock of geese spread out before them. They spent two days, staying overnight at Little Stoke Farm, watching the geese: there were six different varieties present in a flock of 2,000. Amongst these were many White-fronted Geese, a common enough species there in the winter. It was Howard who first spotted that one, a slightly smaller bird, had an unusual thin golden ring around its eyes, but otherwise looked similar. It was a rare Lesser White-fronted Goose, only the second ever to have been recorded in Britain — the

*1936: The old Duck Decoy at Slimbridge.*

*Summer 1944: The pill-box overlooking the Dumbles. It was from this spot that the first of two Lesser White-fronted geese were identified on December 16th 1945.*

first was in Northumberland in 1886. They watched it for half an hour. This was a defining moment. They searched further and from behind the bank, overlooking different parts of the Dumbles, eventually finding a second bird. They checked carefully that it was not the same bird seen twice. Peter Scott had previously considered the possibility that this species was not quite as rare as had been supposed. He was right, a few of the smaller variants would join the flock of their larger, more common cousins. The idea of a future home attached to a wildfowl reserve, there at Slimbridge, took root in Peter Scott's mind on that day, December 16th 1945.

A lasting friendship ensued, and my father became a founder member of the Trust, serving on its Council from the start, later becoming a trustee (Appendix 8). Ten years on and fully established, it was given the distinction of a second Royal visit. Other reserves were opened in different parts of the country, the most recent being the Wildlife and Wetlands reserve at Barnes in London. As an organisation the Trust became famous internationally in the field of conservation, a reputation it still holds.

*December 16th 1945: Leaving for Slimbridge from Little Stoke Farm. Left: Peter Scott, right: Howard Davis, centre: Clive Wilson.*

*A sketch made, on a scrap of paper, by Peter Scott during the visit to Slimbridge on December 16th 1945, highlighting the distinguishing features of a Lesser White-fronted goose.*

*A sketch of the head of a Lesser White-fronted goose drawn in Howard Davis's signed copy of Sir Peter Scott's autobiography* The Eye of the Wind.

Peter Scott was one of many leading ornithologists who visited and stayed on the farm at Little Stoke. The internationally renowned American, Roger Tory Peterson, author of *Birds over America* (amongst many other books) was another. Like Sir Peter Scott, he was an artist as well as an ornithologist, and had agreed to illustrate a newly planned book, *The Field Guide to the Birds of Britain and Europe*. He stayed at the farm to consult my father on the accuracy of many of his bird illustrations. On another occasion Lord Allenbrooke, who had been Chief of the Imperial General Staff in the latter part of the Second World War and keen studier

*Above: Slimbridge Royal visit in 1956. Howard Davis, partly hidden, is 9th from the right.*
*Below: the Wildlife and Wetlands Reserve as it is today.*

of birds, was a welcome guest. He had recently accepted an invitation to become President of the newly formed Trust at Slimbridge. Others, less in the public eye, also stayed. It was, in all, like a golden sunset that lasted for more than ten years in the life of Little Stoke Farm.

I remember my father's account of the interruption of a Trust meeting at Slimbridge, in the early days, when a shotgun was heard. Matters were briefly adjourned, and those present set off in different directions to discover who might be shooting the wildfowl. One was the actor and ornithologist James Robertson Justice. He was a big man with a beard and, when he chose to use it, a thundering voice. He could put the fear of God into anyone, even more so in the twilight gloom. It was he that chose the path that crossed that of the luckless poacher. Quite what exchange took took place is lost in the shadows of history, but it was felt that poacher was unlikely to search for his future meals in and around the Dumbles ever again.

By the early 1960s Howard Davis had served on the Council of the Wildfowl Trust all the years that its rules allowed. Sir Peter was very keen that his close friend should continue to have a role in the trust's affairs, and, in June 1963, he wrote to Howard proposing that he became a trustee, which would entitle him to attend meetings of the Council, with voting rights. His letter ended '...*I was not at all happy at the prospect of breaking a connection so deeply rooted in the origins of the Trust. So this seems a happy solution of the problem with which I very much hope you will agree*'. Of course he did agree and became a trustee until his health determined otherwise.

*   *   *

The house at Clapton in Gordano had a wonderful large garden, partly woodland, that attracted many songbirds, but in the end it was too much for my parents to maintain. They moved to a new house in Winscombe in Somerset, but my father suffered an illness in 1970, and they moved again, to a flat overlooking the River Avon in Sneyd Park in Bristol. Even there some of the ornithological work continued, but on the January 2nd 1974, Howard Davis died peacefully at home, aged but 75 years. A life that had enriched others had, indeed, been fulfilled.

*   *   *   *   *

# Epilogue

## Sir Peter Scott's Tribute to Howard Davis
## at Almondsbury Church
## January 7th 1974

Perhaps it was more of a coincidence than anything else — or perhaps it wasn't — the letter that set in train a sequence which altered the whole pattern of my life, and has made me, for 28 years, deeply grateful to the man who wrote it.

In 1945 Howard Davis wrote to me, 'out of the blue', telling me about the wild geese that spent each winter at the New Grounds on the Severn Estuary, and how they had fared during the war that had just ended. Not long before the war I had been to see the geese there, and he knew that I'd be interested. He said that if I wanted to see them again he'd be ready to take me to the best place for watching them. And so, on a day in December 1945 we met on the canal bridge at Slimbridge, and spent the two days of a weekend watching geese. On the second day it was Howard who first spotted a Lesser White-fronted Goose — only the second official record for the species in Britain — the first having been in 1886. Later in the day we spotted a second Lesser White-front, and altogether seven species of geese were present in the flock. For me it was a momentous day. I had made up my mind that Slimbridge would be the ideal place to set up the Bird Organisation I had been dreaming of all through the war. And so it has proved. A year later Howard Davis was one of five people who met at Shepherd's Patch at Slimbridge to form The Wildfowl Trust, and who became the first members of its Council. As Council Member, and later as Trustee, he served the Wildfowl Trust enthusiastically and loyally for 27 years. I am deeply grateful for his help and encouragement during that time — and there were early days when the organisation passed through very difficult times. But there's something which makes me even more grateful for that letter of long ago. It is that Slimbridge, as some of you will know, is my home. I have no other, and I love it greatly. That too I owe to my old friend Howard Davis.

In the days I have been talking about, Howard was farming at Little Stoke — and a very successful farmer he was — but his heart was in his interest in nature, and particularly birds: and being the responsible man he was, he became involved in the organisation of many other societies besides the Wildfowl Trust. Perhaps his most important service was to the Bristol Naturalists' Society, which he had joined in 1932. From 1937-1953 he was Hon. Secretary of its Ornithological Section and later its President. He first became President of the Parent Society for the years 1950 and 51. The Bristol Naturalists' Society honoured him again in 1962 by electing him President during the Society's Centenary year. He was elected an Hon. Life Member two years later.

He was also a Vice-President of the Ornithological Section of the Somerset Archaeological and Natural History Society, and was elected an Hon. Life Member of that too.

To give you some idea of his range of energetic activity in the field of Wild Life and Natural History, he served on governing bodies of the British Trust for Ornithology, the Royal Society for the Protection of Birds, the British Ornithologists' Union, the Gloucestershire Trust for Nature Conservation and the Somerset Trust for Nature Conservation. He was a founder member of the last two, and he was also a member of the Fauna Preservation Society, the Fair Isle Bird Observatory, and, for a period, of the Zoological Society of London.

I think it is worth mentioning how much these many societies have achieved, not only in providing education and recreation for vast numbers of people, but also in saving for future generations the natural world which holds so much of significance for human survival. Many are active in essential research, and most of them in conservation. Howard's participation in these activities was, I believe, important for their success. Having sat with him round a table for so many years, I can say that his contribution to such work, was always wise, constructive and practical.

In the last few years he was afflicted, as most of you will know, with Parkinson's Disease, and probably only his family can really measure the degree of fortitude he displayed in coming to terms with that illness. I only talked once with him about it and was amazed at his courage and good cheer in face of it. And now, on 2nd January, in his 76th year, he has died - of a heart attack which was perhaps merciful, as he did not have to endure the final stages of his long illness.

All of those of us who knew him must feel enriched by having done so. I like to remember him best when we were excitedly watching wild geese together; and I am happy to have had this opportunity to pay my tribute to the memory of a fine man and a greatly valued friend.

*Bookplate designed by Sir Peter Scott for
Howard Davis.*

*Summer scene on the farm in the 1950s.*

### Notes about Ernest Bucknall (see colour pages).

*Ernest Pile Bucknall was born in Liverpool in 1861; his parents having moved there from the Bristol and Bath area. He grew up to become a sculptor, portrait and landscape painter. His work was exhibited mainly in the south east of England and also in Clifton in 1919. He and his wife Blanche lived their twilight years in south Gloucestershire, both dying in 1935. In the early 1930s he visited Little Stoke Farm at least twice, painting the pictures shown in the colour section.*

# Appendices

# Appendix 1

## The Manors of Stoke Gifford, Harry Stoke and Walls in the mid-1300s

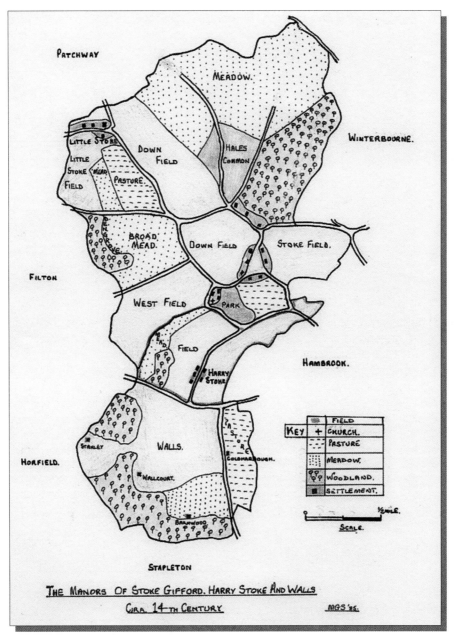

*Open field system in Stoke Gifford in the mid-1300s. Researched by Mike Stanbrook and reproduced with his permission.*

# Appendix 2

## 1471-83 Petition by Sybille Forster: transcription with original spellings

To my Lorde Prince

mekely besecheth youre highnesse youre right humble Orattors and homagors[1] Humphrey /
   Forster Squyer and Sybille his wyf late wyf of Rob[er]t Poyntz Squyer that where

youre saide Orators in right of the sayde Sybille wer seased[2] of estat of Fee of a tenement in /
   Stoke Gyfford other wyse callyd Litill Stoke in the Countie of Glowcester

with certeyn lande mede and pasture to the saide tenement bilonging beying of the yerly value /
   XL l[3] And so ther of seased perceyved the issue and profits of the same by many

yers pesibly and contynually bute now late that youre saide Orators by Wyll{a}m Birkeley of Uley /
   in the saide countie forcibly and ryettysly[4] wer ther of dissesed and there Ferm[er]s

and occupiers ther of fro[m] the same by might of the saide Will{a}m wer expellyd and amovyd /
   which Will{a}m by his saide might wrongfully wyth owte any juste cause or

tytle yet holdeth and occupieth the same agenst whom your saide Orators may have no spedy /
   remedy by the laws of the lande considering that the saide Will{a}m in the saide

Countie of Glowcester of grate might And yo[ur] saide Orators not inhabited in that countie /
   but fer from there wherfor that it may please youre noble g[ra]ce in aide of a com-

plythement of duwe justice and for the spedy relef of youre saide Orators of and for the saide /
   wrongs directe your gray[ci]ous letters myssive to the saide Will{a}m commanding

hym by the same to appiere byfore youre right honorable and to dyscrete councell at a c[er]teyn /
   day to be lymytted therto Answer to the saide compleynts and to shew his title if he

any have yn the premysses and if he refuse so to do than that farther directions be taken by /
   youre saide honorable councell as shalbe thought most according to right witnesse and

for the spedy relef of youre saide Orators and homagors in this behalve at the rev[er]ence of god /
   and in way of charete

\* \* \*

*Letters in [ ] are missing in the original document. See page 126 for a version with modern spelling and
some added punctuation.*

*(1) Orators and homagors: Petitioners      (2) Seased (seised): in lawful possession of…*
*(3) Symbol after 40 is unclear: 'l' (£) or 's' (shilling). £40 p.a. is a more typical income for a Squire.*
*(4) Ryettysly: riotously*

# 1471-83 Petition by Sybil Forster: transcription with modern spellings

To my Lord Prince

meekly beseech your highness your right humble Orators and homagers Humphrey Forster /
    Squire and Sybil, his wife, late wife of Robert Poyntz Squire, that were

your said Orators in right of the said Sybil were seised of estate of fee of a tenement in Stoke /
    Gifford otherwise called Little Stoke in the County of Gloucester

with certain land, meadow and pasture to the said tenement belonging, being of the yearly /
    value 40£. And so thereof seised, perceived the issue and profits of the same by many

years peaceably and continually, but now late that your said Orators, by William Berkeley of Uley /
    in the said county, forcibly and riotously were thereof deseised and their Farmers

and occupiers thereof from the same, by might of the said William were expelled and removed, /
    which William, by his said might wrongfully, without any just cause or

title, yet holds and occupies the same against whom your said Orators may have no speedy /
    remedy by the laws of the land considering that the said William in the said

County of Gloucester of great might. And your said Orators not inhabited in that county but far /
    from there, wherefore that it may please your noble grace in aide of com-

pliance of due justice and for the speedy relief of your said Orators of and for the said wrongs, /
    to direct your gracious letters missive to the said William commanding

him by the same to appear before your right honorable and to discrete council at a certain day to /
    be limited there to answer to the said complaints and to show his title if he

any have in the premises, and, if he do, then that further directions be taken by /
    your said honorable council as shall be thought most according to right witness and

for the speedy relief of your said Orators and homagers in this behalf at the reverence of god and /
    in way of charity.

*(Transcriptions by the author)*

# Appendix 3

## Extracts from the 1649 survey of the five farms at Little Stoke.

The survey was carried out for the Berkeleys by Richard Lawford, of Stoke Gifford, probably the brother of Thomas Lawford, who later occupied the main farm at Little Stoke.

The survey lists the five farms and names the fields attached to each tenant. Assuming the location of the farms is the same as in the later 1725 survey, a comparison of field name enables a tentative link to be made between the 1649 tenants and the farms shown on the 1725 map — see pages 11 and 12.

| The 1649 farm of | | The 1725 farm of |
|---|---|---|
| Robert Larence | became | Samuel Tyson |
| Richard Driner | became | Mrs Freeman |
| Thomas Focham | became | Thomas Baylis |
| Beth Smyth | became | Mr Duckenfield |
| Israell Holbrow | became | John Harris |

Many fields had the same names in 1649 and 1725, often with different spellings.

Robert Larence his tenement

The house backside Corthard being one akere$
of ground ———————————————— } 02 — 00

One ground called the home close being
7 akeres of ground att ——————————— } 03 — 00

One ground called Long lands being 12 —
akeares of ground; on the south side of } 09 — 00
the house ——————————————————

one meddow ground called land meade —
being 5 akeares of ground Ioyning — } 05 — 00
to little stokes meade att ——————

Two akeares & ahalfe in littell stokes meade 02 — 10
one halfe akeare in brode meade att —— 00 — 10

One ground called new lease being 4 akeres$
of ground lying on the east side of the house } 03 — 00

Two grounds called Downe feald being 7
akeares of ground Ioyning to the same } 05 — 00

One ground called Mattfords being in
severall partes; lying beyond the same;
and 18 akeares of ground 3 of it being } 14 — 00
stone meade att ——————————————

Sum is — 44 — 00 — 00

The entry in the 1649 Survey for Robert Larence (Lawrence) who farmed 53 acres (valued at £44) from a house and farm buildings on the site of the much enlarged single Little Stoke Farm created some 150 years later. Most of the field names, but not their spellings, are the same as in 1725.

# Field names in 1649 and 1725

| Robert Larence's holding 1649 | Samuel Tyson's holding 1725 |
|---|---|
| House & Orchard | House, Garden & Orchard |
| Home Close | Home Close [161] |
| Long Lands | Upper Longmead [255] |
| | Lower Longmead [248] |
| Land Meade | Land Mead [234] |
| Littell Stokes Meade (*part of*) | — |
| Brode Meade (*part of*) | — |
| New Lease | New Leas [279] |
| Dowene Fealde (*2 fields*) | Great Downfield [277] |
| | Little Downfield [280] |
| Mattfords (*2 fields*) | Great Mattford [329] |
| | Little Mattford [328] |
| Stone Meade | Great Sandy Close [341] |
| | Little Sandy Close [342] |

*The numbers are the original field numbers on the 1725 survey map.*

In the 1725 survey the parts of Little Stoke Mead and Broad Mead were not within Samuel Tyson's tenancy.

# Appendix 4

1. Little Stoke Farm tenants from 1799, from Badminton House Records.

ESTATE OFFICE,

BADMINTON,

GLOUCESTERSHIRE.

17th March, 1927.

Dear Sir,

    In reply to your letter of the 14th inst., I have looked up the records and I find that from 1799 onwards the tenants of Little Stoke Farm were as follows:-

| | |
|---|---|
| 1799. | Benjamin Dowling. |
| 1812 | Thomas Hulbert. |
| 1815. | Wm. Willcox. |
| 1822. | Widow Willcox. |
| 1829. | Hannah Willcox. |
| 1854. | Benjamin Willcox. |
| 1886. | Benjamin Willcox and Sydney B. Witchell. |
| 1892. | Sydney B. Witchell. |
| 1896. | E. K. Davis. |

    If there is any further information you wish as to the tenancies., I shall be glad to look it up.

Yours faithfully,

*John Poole.*

P.S.

*I remember Wm Henry Davis very well.*

Mr. E. K. Davis,

*Badminton Estate letter in reply to a query by Edward Davis in 1927.*

2. Stoke Gifford farms 1789 to 1915, showing the gradual reduction in number as the surviving farms grew larger through amalgamation

### 1789 (11 farms)

Bailey's Court Farm  -  William Builder
Cobb's & Harris's Farm  -  Edward Gunter
Coldharbour Farm  -  William Bawn
Court Farm  -  Edward Bawn
Field Farm  -  Samuel & William Tyler
Harry Stoke Farm  -  Thomas Nichols
Laffords (Knightwood) Farm  -  William Turner
Little Stoke Farm  -  Benjamin Dowling
Walls Court Farm  -  Joseph Esmand
Watch Elm Farm  -  William Blinman
Woodhouse Farm  -  W. & D. Webb:

### 1850 (10 farms)

Bailey's Court Farm  -  William Hooper
Coldharbour Farm  -  John Parker (jnr)
Court Farm and Watch Elm Farm (part of)  -  Joseph Parker
Field Farm  -  Richard B. Witchell
Harry Stoke Farm  -  Robert Andrews
Laffords (Knightwood) Farm  -  Joseph Limbrick
Little Stoke Farm  -  Hannah (Widow) Willcox
Walls Court Farm  -  (No name)
Watch Elm Farm (part of )  -  Thomas Sherbourne
Woodhouse Farm  -  Thomas E. Webb

### 1915 (8 farms)

Bailey's Court Farm  -  Mr E. Pursey
Coldharbour Farm  -  J. P. Parker
Court Farm  -  Mr Thomas Pierce
Harry Stoke Farm  -  Mr Charles Bridgeman
Knightwood Farm  -  Mr A. H. Beauchamp
Little Stoke Farm  -  Mr E. H. K. Davis
Stanley Farm  -  G. W. & A. E.  Mortimer
Walls Court  -  G. W. & A. E.  Mortimer and J P Parker

# Appendix 5

Little Stoke Farm plans, 1856

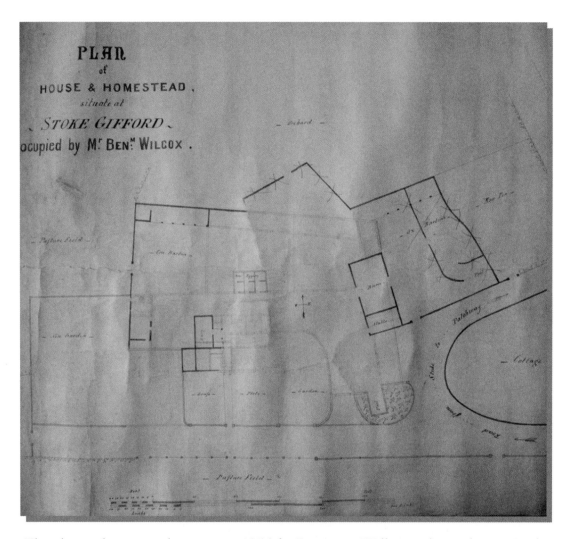

The above plans were drawn up in 1856 for Benjamin Willcox, who took over Little Stoke Farm on his mother's death in 1852. The plans are not supported by notes or additional sketches: their interpretation will include some degree of speculation. The dark solid lines must show the main existing features: some, with pencilled crosses were to be demolished. New buildings are in faint lines. Right of centre is the barn/stable, which shows up on the 1725 survey map (page 11), forming part of

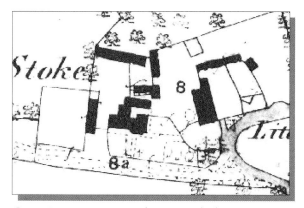

Thomas Baylis's farm. His house once stood just above the words 'Ox Barton' on the above plan.

On the left is a detail from the 1881 Ordnance Survey map. Comparison with the 1856 plans shows the extent of the actual alterations made. The two walls in Ox Barton were retained, while the cowsheds at the top of Cow Barton were only extended part way across the top of the next yard. The next section was rotated to run north-south and a stable was built next to the three new pigsties.

*The three pigsties in 1943.*

*Front of the barn in 1943.*

*Rear of the barn (1943).*

*'Ox Barton' (1943)*

Internally the 1856 plans show all the ground floor rooms that existed a century later. The organisation of the garden in 1881 shows three sections as in the 1856 plans, but the farm entrance in 1881 was in the same place as in 1950s, not as in the original 1856 plans.

# Appendix 6

## 1. Farm sale details, 1853: Following the death of Hannah Willcox

Comparing this with the later sales in 1896 and 1956 provides interesting clues about the changes in farming methods over the 100-year period.

From advertisement columns (Sales by Auction) of the

<u>Bristol Mercury</u>
Western Counties, Monmouthshire and South Wales Advertiser
Saturday, March 12th, 1853

STOKE GIFFORD
Five miles from Bristol, on the Gloucester Road.
IMPORTANT SALE OF FARMING STOCK.
MESSRS J. TAYLOR AND SON are instructed to sell by
AUCTION, on MONDAY next, March 14th and two following
days, commencing each day at Eleven o'clock.
The whole of the live and Dead FARMING STOCK, CORN,
HAY, ROOTS, IMPLEMENTS HOUSEHOLD FURNITURE, and
other effects, of Mrs Willcox, deceased:
Comprising 63 head of horned cattle, 235 sheep, cart and
nag horses, store pigs, ten ricks of wheat and oats, six mows of
hay, about 100 tons of roots, complete sets of farming implements,
and dairy and brewing utensils, apple mill and press; also the
whole of the Household Furniture.
Further particulars in handbills and in Catalogues.

Westbury-on-Trym, March, 1853.

## 2. Farm sale details, 1896:  Following the death of Sidney B. Witchell

From the advertisement columns (Sale by Auction) of the

### *Bristol Times and Mirror*
Saturday, March 28, 1896

VERY HIGHLY IMPORTANT SALE OF LIVE AND DEAD FARMING STOCK

LITTLE STOKE FARM, GLOUCESTERSHIRE

Close to Patchway Station

GEO. NICHOLS, SMITH and ALDER

Have received instructions from the Executrix of the late Mr S. B. Witchell to SELL by AUCTION on the premises on TUESDAY next, March 31, 1896.

82 Head of well bred HORNED CATTLE, 126 Crossbred SHEEP, 9 powerful CART HORSES, COB, 15 PIGS, Agricultural IMPLEMENTS, DAIRY UTENSILS, STRAW (to go off), OATS, CIDER, etc., comprising:

HORNED CATTLE — 2 capital dairy cows and calves, 12 cows and heifers, fresh steers, 2 coming three-year-old steers, 27 well-bred coming two-year-old ditto, 12 yearling ditto, 12 weaned calves.

SHEEP — 43 cross bred double and single couples, 4 barren ewes, 10 fat sheep, 68 cross bred tegs, two-toothed ram.

HORSES — 9 powerful cart geldings and mares, handsome cob, six years old, 14 hands.

AGRICULTURAL IMPLEMENTS, ETC. — 5 wagons, 4 broad-wheel carts, narrow wheel ditto, spring ditto, 4 wheel dog cart, pony trap, 2 mowing machines, 3 tedding ditto, 2 horse rakes, corn drill, root ditto, 3 iron ploughs, skim ditto, scarifier, horse hoe, set of drags and harrows, Cambridge ring roller, iron ditto, several covered sheep racks and troughs, root pulper, cake crusher, chaff machine, horse gear, turnip cutter, winnowing machine, large hay rack, cattle cribs, weighing machine and weights, ladders, and hay knives, cider casks, iron and wooden hurdles, cider mill and cloths, grind stones, corn bins, agricultural tools, barrel churn (by Hathaway), milk lead, milk coolers and stands, butter trendle, scales and weights, and sundries.

About 50 QRS BLACK TARTAR OATS, 6 ricks of TIED WHEAT STRAW, and 2000 gals. of prime CIDER in convenient lots; also several lots of

## HOUSEHOLD FURNITURE

Comprising rosewood round table, piano, chiffonniere and numerous sundries.

The horned cattle are particularly well bred, with excellent coats and good colour, and all out-lyers; the slips are in good condition, Horses powerful and good workers, the implements modern and in good condition.

LUNCHEON AT 11 O'CLOCK, 1s EACH

SALE AT 12 PRECISELY

## 3. Farm valuation details, 1956: On the retirement of Howard Davis

*Note: The information below has been extracted from the sale details, which cover many pages. It is only a summary of the main items that are helpful when comparing this with the sales in 1853 and 1896*

Horses:
"Blossom" — aged, quite good in all gears

Cattle:
Dairy cattle: 64; Barren cows and heiffers: 7; Heifers with calves at foot or in calf: 11; Young cattle 24; Calves: 8

Pigs:
Wessex Saddleback and litter of 11; Litter of 11 Large White slip pigs; Litter of 8 Saddleback slips; 5 Large White store pigs

Implements:
Barford and Perkins Cake crusher; Winnowing machine; Bartlett platform scales and weights; Single harrow and drill; Set of zig-zag harrows; Set of hay drags; Disc harrow; Set of spike harrows; Martin 9 tine cultivator; Flat roller; Triple ring roller; Cambridge ring roller; Two 2 furrow ploughs; One skim plough; Denning Somerset disc corn drill; Mowing machine; Massey Harris mowing machine; McCormick International green crop loader; Bambford combine swathe turner; Nicholson's tedding machine; 2 horse rakes; A 9 tine hay sweep; Lister engine; Wallis-Titt elevator; Massey Harris 5ft cut binder; Fordson Standard Tractor (1941); Fordson Diesel Tractor (1954); 5 trailers with ladders; plus a large quantity of smaller sundry items.

# Appendix 7

## Air raids, 1940

In chapter 4 reference was made to four of the many raids that affected the area around Stoke Gifford, Patchway and Filton. These have been extensively researched by John Penny, author of *Bristol at War*. The following has been distilled from his extensive research notes.

### Saturday Night 17th/18th August 1940

During the night enemy aircraft, most operating singly, carried out raids over Wales and in many districts of England west of a line from Preston to Canterbury. Many of the bombs fell in rural areas with little effect, but damage was caused at Liverpool, Birmingham and Swansea.

The night raiders included the fourteen Heinkel He 111s based at Bourges-Avord, which took off between 20.00 and 24.00 hrs to attack the Bristol Aeroplane Company at Filton, Rolls-Royce at Crewe, and the airfields at Sealand and Penhros, flying in over the coast from 22.00 hrs between Weymouth and Exmouth. The weather was fine, with a brilliant moon, and eleven raids crossed and re-crossed the Bristol area between 22.40 and 02.52 hrs at altitudes of between 11,000 and 20,000 feet. A number of bombs was dropped in South Gloucestershire and North Somerset.

Incidents in South Gloucestershire:

This area bore the brunt of the local attack and, between 22.45 and 02.00 hrs, some 46 high explosives (HE), including 18 unexploded bombs (UXB), were dropped. *Patchway*: 23.50 hrs, damage reported at Callicroft Road, Gipsy Patch Lane, and Gloucester Road. *Pilning*: 01.47 hrs, at Rookery Farm 14 HEs and a UXB demolished two houses, damaged power cables, and killed a horse. *Filton*: 6 UXBs (5 x 50 kg and 1 x 250 kg) fell on the airfield damaging the night runway, which was under construction at that time. Incidents were also reported during the night at Almondsbury, Charlton, Berwick Wood, East Hallen, Stoke Gifford and Little Stoke.

### Thursday Night 22nd/23rd August 1940

During the night German activity was on a larger scale and more widespread than for some time, and in addition to an attack on the Bristol Aeroplane Company there were raids in Liverpool and the South Midlands. Bombs also fell in Cardiff, Newhaven and the northern suburbs of London.

The 23 Heinkel He 111s dispatched to Filton took off from Vannes-Meuçon between 21.00 and 00.32 hrs, the aircraft first being detected near Cherbourg flying on a northerly course. All the raids except one flew in over Weymouth and Portland direct to Bristol, the exception crossing the coast in Devon and flying up the Bristol Channel to Avonmouth. Locally there was clear moonlight up to 02.00 hrs, after which some cloud developed at 10,000 feet.

The Filton attackers were the next to arrive between 22.47 and 02.47 hrs, during which time some 21 raids were tracked at altitudes of between 15,000 and 30,000 feet, and ten of these were illuminated by the searchlights from 22.51 until 00.35 hrs. Hostile action occurred in South Gloucestershire and North Somerset before the last intruder was plotted flying back across the area at 04.28 hrs. During the night, however, only five raids were positively identified as having dropped bombs, all having been illuminated by searchlights.

Incidents in South Gloucestershire:-

A total of 168 HE and 250 incendiary bombs (IB) were reported in the Almondsbury, Aust, Filton, Patchway and Stoke Gifford districts.

*Filton & Patchway:* The Bristol Aeroplane Company works was attacked three times between 23.18 and 02.45 hrs., during which time about 30 HEs and a number of IBs were reported, 13 or 14 of these falling on B.A.C. premises. Considerable damage was caused to the works, in particular at No.4 Factory and No.11 Test Bed, both south of Gipsy Patch Lane. While bombs were still falling, Frederick Ernest Rose, a maintenance engineer in charge of a salvage party, led two assistants into damaged buildings and, hampered by flood water and darkness, extinguished fires which had started in a store of magnesium. He then led his men to help check fires which had started in another area, and for his bravery was later awarded the George Medal. Gipsy Patch Lane was blocked, and a water main, a gas main and electricity cables were damaged. 20 HEs fell in fields near Patchway railway station, and some 250 IBs were also reported. 6 houses in the area were badly damaged, with roofs, garages and outbuildings suffering, while windows were broken over a wide area. In addition, 6 UXBs were later found at Hempton Court Farm. Total casualties in the area amounted to 2 seriously and 2 slightly injured. *Stoke Gifford & Little Stoke:* During 3 raids between 23.15 hrs. and 00.07 hrs 33 HEs and one UXB were dropped near Stoke Gifford and 10 HEs between Stoke Gifford and Patchway, two unoccupied houses being demolished at Little Stoke Estate. *Almondsbury:* 6 UXBs were reported, and the Memorial Hall was half demolished. Six women ambulance workers and three messenger boys sheltering in the cellar under the stage were unharmed. Two fires were also started in the village and damage caused to electricity cables while three roads, including the A38, were partly blocked. *Aust:* 9 UXBs fell damaging a cottage and an inn, cracking the church tower, and blocking the B4055 road.

## Wednesday Night 4th/5th September 1940

During the night enemy bombers were very active, with Liverpool as the main target. Other raiders made for Bristol, South Wales and the Thames Estuary, and bombing was reported in Salford, Tilbury, Stoke on Trent, Bournemouth, Bristol, as well as in rural areas of Kent, Sussex, Somerset and Gloucestershire. The night raiders included 48 aircraft which bombed the Bristol area, this attack force comprised 25 Heinkel He 111s in and 23 Junkers Ju 88s.

From about 21.00 hrs a continuous stream of aircraft flew in from Cherbourg, crossing the English coast between Portland and the Isle of Wight. Most flew due north to Liverpool, while others took a more westerly course to the Bristol Channel and South Wales. Most aircraft returned by a similar route, crossing the coast between Portland and Selsey Bill in the direction of Cherbourg. Three raids, however, came in between Lyme Bay and the Lizard, flying to the Bristol Channel and South Wales, and mine laying was suspected in the Bristol Channel.

Locally, the sky was perfectly clear until the early hours of the morning when a ground mist arose, which was particularly heavy in certain localities, and between 21.21 and 04.53 hrs. 53 raids were plotted in the Bristol area flying in from the south and south-east. Bombs fell in Bristol, South Gloucestershire and North Somerset. Many of the raids were illuminated by the searchlights, the enemy responding in some cases by firing down the searchlight beams.

Incidents in South Gloucestershire:-

*Filton:* At 21.41 hrs the Bristol Aeroplane Company reported an HE and an OB affecting No.2 shop and 120 machines in the gear shop, and 24 machines in the tool room were affected by damage to the electricity and water supplies, but production was not interrupted. *Frampton Cotterell:* 15 HEs at Frampton End killed chickens and damaged electricity supplies. An HE in School Road blocked the road and extensively damaged the Cross Hands Inn. There was also minor damage to houses and telephone cables. *Harry Stoke:* Four UXBs reported. Winterbourne: Four HEs were reported, followed by a further 22 HEs and an oil bomb (OB) at French Lane, Northwoods. *Pucklechurch:* Three HEs and an OB at Hodden Lane caused minor damage to a house. *Abson:* Two HEs and an OB reported. *Easter Compton:* Six HEs and a UXB slightly damaged a storehouse. *Pilning:* 24.00 hrs, nine HEs fell at the Cross Hands, and a further four HEs and three OBs came down at Poplar Farm. Two houses were demolished, one extensively damaged, many suffered minor damage, and electricity supplies interrupted. One man was slightly injured. *Almondsbury:* 00.25 hrs, six HEs fell at Hortham Colony and Woodlands Farm, and 17 HEs and two OBs at Upper Kempton Farm, "Oaklands", Hill Farm, and Brothers Wood Farm. *Alveston:* An OB fell at Conygre Farm, Shellard's Lane. *Badminton:* Eight HEs and two UXBs reported. *Hawkesbury:* 12 HEs and an OB dropped between the church and Cold Change Hill, blocking two roads. *West Littleton:* An OB fell at Home Farm, and 22 HEs and an OB at West Farm.

## Wednesday 25th September 1940

At 09.50 hrs a single reconnaissance aircraft came in over Warmwell and flew up to the northwest of Glastonbury, where it was plotted at 10.03 hrs. It then turned west and flying at an altitude of 25,000 feet turned back, finally exiting to the west of Portland.

The main target of this daytime raid was the Bristol Aeroplane Company and a total of 136 Heinkel He 111s were dispatched to Filton. To assist the main attack force 51 Messerschmitt Bf 109s, flying from Beaumont le Roger, and from airstrips on Guernsey and Brittany provided short range fighter protection over the English Channel. In addition, 52 Messerschmitt Bf 110s from Cherbourg, Le Havre, and Thiberville, escorted the bombers to and from the target.

At 11.24 hrs, 50+ enemy aircraft were plotted off the Dorset coast near Portland arriving from Cherbourg, before flying on to Dorchester, Yeovil, Castle Cary, Weston super Mare, Avonmouth, Filton and Wotton under Edge, after which they turned due south and finally flew out over Swanage. To counter it a total of 41 fighters were scrambled, these being the 14 Spitfires of No. 609 Squadron and twelve Hurricanes of No. 238 Squadron, both based at Middle Wallop, in addition to the twelve Spitfires of Warmwell's No. 152 Squadron and the three Hurricanes of 'Red Section', No. 601 Squadron from Exeter. As the Westland Aircraft works at Yeovil was at first thought to be the likely target, the fighters were initially sent to that area. The raiders, however, by-passed Yeovil, flying north in a tight arrow head formation in the direction of Cardiff, and only No. 152 Squadron engaged them before they reached the Bristol area.

On reaching the Bristol Channel coast at Weston super Mare the attack force turned north east, the rear aircraft taking up a very wide circle, before forming up behind, thus making two formations about half a mile apart. Still in a tight arrowhead form these two waves continued on towards Bristol flying at between 15,400 and 19,000 feet, and after, turning in towards Filton.

The remaining bombers carried out a high level attack on the premises of the Bristol Aeroplane Company at 11.45 hrs, the weather in the area being perfect for bombing, with banks of thick clouds broken by patches of clear blue sky. After attacking, the raiders turned for home, and on the return flight were at last fully engaged by the R.A.F. fighters, as well as by the Holton Heath anti-aircraft guns at 12.06 hrs, before flying out over Swanage.

Eight German aircraft failed to make it back across the English Channel. On the British side, in addition to the Spitfire from No.152 Squadron in which Sergeant Kenneth Holland-Ripley lost his life, the squadron suffered three other aircraft damaged in combat.

Incidents in the South Gloucestershire:-

*Filton*: 11.48 hrs, 168 HEs fell on B.A.C. property within 45 seconds when enemy aircraft flew over the works. The majority was of a large calibre, making craters about 15 feet to 30 feet in diameter, but many OBs were also used. There were also 50 or more UXBs reported, but many of these turned out to be delayed action bombs (DABs), which exploded a few hours later, most in or near the B.A.C. works. Clifford Bruce Dunning, A.R.P. Plotting Officer at Bristol, immediately volunteered to undertake the dangerous work of examining and reporting all such suspect UXBs with a view to furnishing his H.Q. with accurate information concerning them. He was examining the UXBs, and left one to be dealt with by the disposal party before moving on to another not far distant when within minutes the first exploded. Luckily he was far enough away to escape injury; though fragments of the exploding bomb and debris flew all around him. Dunning visited and reported on a large number of bombs, both then and during later attacks, and the information given by him was of the greatest value. For the courage he displayed in voluntarily undertaking such highly dangerous work during subsequent raids, but more especially for his efforts on the 25th, Dunning was awarded the George Medal in Marcch 1941.

The Rodney Works were seriously damaged, and here and at the Flight Shed and the East Engine works a number of underground workers' shelters were hit causing heavy casualties. A large number of HEs also caused considerable damage to Filton village to the south-east of the aeroplane works, and several DABs exploded during the following 24 hours. About 900 houses were damaged and eight demolished, with 400 people being evacuated to 5 hostels, either through their homes being damaged or on account of UXBs. A six inch water main was damaged in addition to a nine inch and a 12 inch gas main. The main Gloucester Road, the A38 and several minor roads were blocked, while incidental damage was caused to electricity and telephone services. The up and down G.W.R. main lines between Filton Junction and Patchway were both temporarily blocked but were being used again for traffic within three hours, although subject to a speed restriction of five mph on approaching the crater. At North Filton both lines were damaged and put out of use for some days. 12 men of the 4th Battalion, The Royal Berkshire Regiment, on a route march along the Gloucester Road between Filton and Patchway, were also killed during the attack, and the total casualties in Filton, (not including the B.A.C. works), amounted to 25 killed and 150 injured. The total killed in Filton as a result of enemy action on 25th September, including those at the B.A.C., was 26.

*Stoke Gifford*: 11.48 hrs, three HEs demolished six houses and damaged a further 26, while gas and electricity mains were also affected. A direct hit was also scored on the Bailey's Court Farm 'Dazzle Defence' searchlight site, where Gunner Arthur Taylor of the 354th Battery, 39th Searchlight Regiment was also killed. The light anti-aircraft defences at Filton, manned by the 73rd Battery 23rd L.A.A. Regiment, also suffered some damage when a hut was hit and a gunner injured. Two cows were also killed and 13 injured, but these were destroyed later. *Winterbourne*: 11.48 hrs, five H.Es fell at Northwood. One house was demolished and a farmhouse damaged.

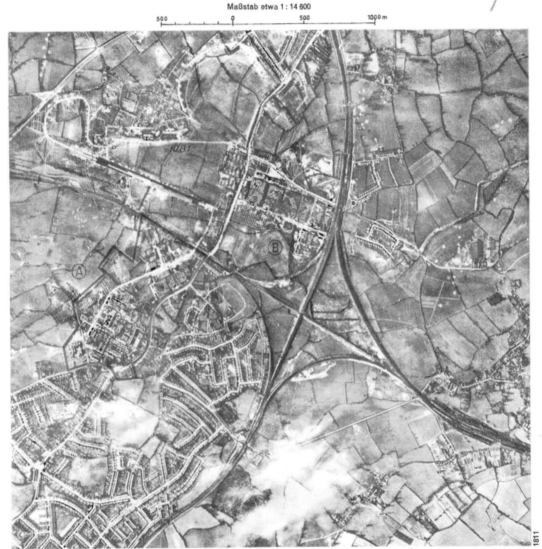

# Filton

### Werk für Flugzeugzellen
### „The Bristol Aeroplane Co. Ltd."

Länge (westl. Greenw.): 2° 34′ 30″   Breite: 51° 30′ 50″
Mißweisung: — 11° 36′ (Mitte 1940)   Zielhöhe über NN 65 m

Maßstab etwa 1 : 14 600

500      0      500      1000 m

Genst. 5. Abt.   November 1940

Karte 1 : 100 000
GB/E 32

(A)   GB 74 52   Werk für Flugzeugzellen „The Bristol Aeroplane Co. Ltd."
(B)   GB 73 52   Flugmotorenfabrik „The Bristol Aeroplane Co. Ltd."

*November 1940: German reconnaissance photograph of the Filton area. Little Stoke Farm covers the top right quarter of the photograph. Note the camouflaged roofs of the shadow factory just above the letter B in the upper centre. Bomb craters are evident in many fields.*

# Defences

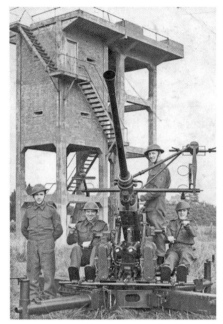

*Bofors gun, crew and tower*          *Barrage balloon*

Heavy anti-aircraft guns were deployed by early September 1939, and although initially operating from temporary sites, by late November were emplaced on permanent positions at various sites surrounding Bristol. By the beginning of June 1940, four 3.7" guns were in place on each site, providing the Bristol area with 24 heavy anti-aircraft guns with which to counter the expected raids, far too few, as it turned out, for so important a target. The anti-aircraft guns were supported by Searchlight units. Dazzle light units were set up to 'blind' the bomber pilots. They were not judged to be effective.

Sir Stanley White, the Managing Director of the Bristol Aeroplane Company, requested that a balloon barrage should be provided to protect the company's works at Filton, despite the difficulties this might cause to fighter aircraft operating from the nearby aerodrome. No.935 Squadron moved immediately from Cardiff to Filton. From the end of May until late September, when a very damaging attack was carried out against the aircraft factories, only a few fighter squadrons were on short term deployment at Filton as the balloon barrage had made the airfield difficult to use as a fighter station by day, and impossible by night. One of the 24 sites covering the Filton area was based in the field opposite the farmhouse at Little Stoke.

Light anti-aircraft guns were set up in various locations, including the Filton area. Some were platform mounted. The picture, above left, shows a Bofors gun prior to its installation on the platform. Such a platform was built in the field behind Rossall Avenue in Little Stoke.

A fighter squadron of Hurricane aircraft was deployed on the Filton airfield immediately after the raids on September 25th 1940.

# Appendix 8

## The Severn Wildfowl Trust

THE SEVERN WILDFOWL TRUST

A meeting was held at the Patch Bridge Guest House,
SLIMBRIDGE, Glos., on Sunday 10th November, 1946.

The following were present:-

Capt. R.G.W. Berkeley.
Michael Bratby, Esq.
H.H. Davis, Esq.
J.R. Justice, Esq.
K. Miller Jones, Esq.
Peter Scott, Esq.

After a short discussion the following Resolution
was put to the meeting:-

That a Society be formed with the name of "The
Severn Wildfowl Trust" and that the draft Rules produced to
the meeting be adopted as the Rules of the Trust.

The Resolution was carried nem. con. and the
proceedings then terminated.

(signed) PETER SCOTT.

*Minutes of the meeting held, on the Patch Bridge Guesthouse, Slimbridge on November 10th 1946, at which the future Severn Wildfowl Trust was founded.*

8 EDWARDES SQUARE LONDON W 8

WESTERN 4079

5th December, 1946.

My Dear Howard,

You will be delighted to hear that
Lord Alanbrooke has accepted the
Presidency of our Trust, and also that
Bernard Tucker is prepared to serve on
our Council. I have also done well, I
think, in getting Sir Archibald Jamieson
the Chairman of Vickers, and a very 'big
noise' in the city, to agree to be our
Treasurer. I have two good candidates
for Secretary, both so excellent, that I
do not know which we should select.

I am bringing my wife down to see
the geese this weekend; I wonder if
you would be there.

Yours ever,

Peter

*Peter Scott's personal letter to Howard Davis about developments in setting up the
Severn Wildfowl Trust.*

*On December 17th 1946 Peter Scott wrote to the members of the Trust's Council,
proposing the following appointments: co-opted to the Council, Bernard W. Tucker
(editor of British Birds), Phyllis Barclay Smith (secretary of the Committee for Bird
Preservation and editor of the Avicultural Magazine); President, Lord Alanbrooke, K.G.,
G.C.B., D.S.O. (former Chief of the Imperial General Staff); Treasurer, Sir Archbald
Jamieson K.B.E (Chairman of Vickers); Secretary, Michael Bratby; Assistant Secretary,
Miss P. Jamieson; Trustee, Lord Kennet of the Dene, P.C., G.B.E., D.S.O., D.S.C.*

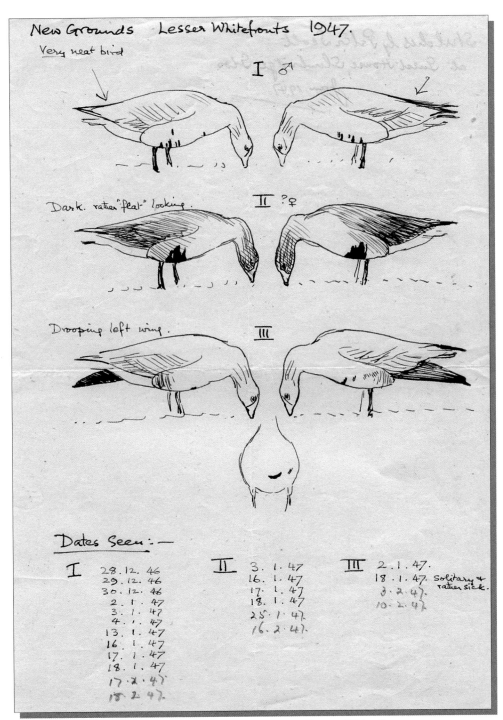

*Sketches made by Peter Scott, illustrating variations in Lesser White-fronts seen at Slimbridge during the winter of 1946/47.*

# Appendix 9

## Modern map of Little Stoke & Bradley Stoke

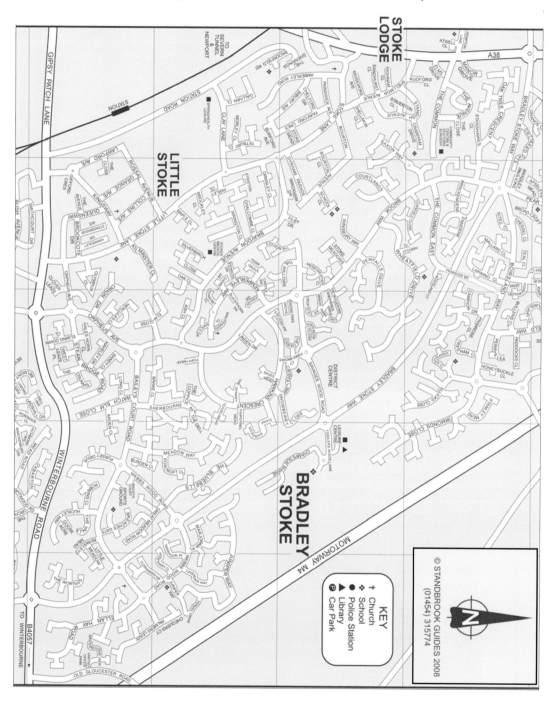

# Postscript

The story of Little Stoke Farm may have caught your imagination for a variety of reasons. You may have personal memories of Little Stoke because you once lived there or nearby. Perhaps you have moved into the area since the modern houses were built, and want a glimpse of what it was once like. You may have associations with one of the other farms listed below; all have vanished. On the other hand you may have no link with South Gloucestershire, but have seen the story of the fate of Little Stoke Farm as a metaphor for the accelerating destruction of rural Britain. In 1896, when my grandfather took over the tenancy of the farm, the edge of Bristol was some four miles to the south, with many flourishing farms on the land in between. Just a few of the farmhouses survive: modern uses having been found for them, but their futures are not secure. Of many others there is no trace. Once those with living memories of them have passed on, a part of our heritage is lost for ever: perhaps a few photographs are all that remains to remind us of the end of a long period during which the landscape gradually evolved.

Twenty two of the farms in the small area shown on the map on page ii have vanished. Perhaps just two survive, protected, for the present by the M4 motorway.

| | | |
|---|---|---|
| Bailey's Court Farm | Bowsland Farm | Callicroft Farm |
| Cherry Rock Farm | Church Farm, Filton [1] | Cobb's and Harris's Farm [2] |
| Coldharbour Farm | Coneygore Farm [3] | Court Farm |
| Field Farm | Hall Farm | Harry Stoke Farm |
| Hayes Farm | Hempton farm, | Knightwood Farm |
| Little Stoke Farm | Manor Farm | Patchway Farm [1] |
| Stanley Farm | Walls Court Farm | Watch Elm Farm [2] |
| Woodhouse Farm [2] | | |

This is just a small fraction of the ever increasing loss of heritage around just one city. Multiplied across the nation, the scale of loss is staggering, but passes almost un-noticed! In southern England expect it to accelerate.

*1: Not specified on the map.*
*2: Incorporated into neighbouring farms in the 19th century, but have since vanished.*
*3: Modern spelling, Conygre.*

# Further Reading

**Stoke Gifford History**

*A Short History of Stoke Gifford and its Parish Church* by D. R. Evans

*A Brief History of Stoke Gifford* by Ros Bromhead. Both are currently out of print

**Websites**

Stoke Gifford Parish Council: www.stokegifford.gov.uk.  A CD about Stoke Gifford, edited by Adrian Kerton, is available through the Parish Council's website.

Adrian Kerton's Stoke Gifford website:
www.adriankweb.pwp.blueyonder.co.uk/History/1_SG_Hist_index_CD2.htm

The National Archives website lists documents relating to Stoke Gifford held by the Gloucestershire Archives.

**Domesday Book**

Pages from the Domesday book can be downloaded from the National Archives. Phillimore has published a series of books covering each county, with details of the Domesday survey: volume 15, published 1982, is about Gloucestershire.

**Medieval landscapes - a selection for further reading**

*The Making of the English Landscape* by W. G. Hoskins, published by Hodder and Stoughton; first published in 1955, revised 1974.

*The Gloucestershire Landscape* by H. P. R. Ginsberg, published by Hodder and Stoughton; first published in 1955, revised 1975.

*Shaping Medieval Landscapes - Settlement, Society, Environment* by Tom Wilkinson, published by Windgather Press, 2005.

*The Landscape of Gloucestershire* by Alan Pilbean, published by Tempus, 2006.

*The Time Traveller's Guide to Medieval England: A Handbook for Visitors to the Fourteenth Century*, by Ian Mortimer, published by Bodley Head, 2008.

**Slimbridge**

*The Eye of the Wind, An Autobiography* by Peter Scott, published by Hodder and Stoughton, 1961.

*Peter Scott, Painter and Naturalist* by Elspeth Huxley, published by Faber and Faber, 1993.

*October 2007: Savages Wood*